*Ultimate
Dim-Mak*

Warning

The techniques and drills depicted in this book are extremely dangerous. It is not the intent of the author or publisher to encourage readers to attempt any of these techniques and drills without proper professional supervision and training. Attempting to do so can result in severe injury or death. Do not attempt any of these techniques or drills without the supervision of a certified instructor.

The author, publisher, and distributors of this book disclaim any liability from any damage or injuries of any type that a reader or user of information contained within this book may encounter from the use of said information. *This book is for information purposes only.*

Ultimate Dim-Mak

How to Fight a Grappler and Win

ERLE MONTAIGUE

PALADIN PRESS • BOULDER, COLORADO

Also by Erle Montaigue:
Advanced Dim Mak: The Finer Points of Death-Point Striking
Baguazhang: Fighting Secrets of the Eight Trigram Palms
Dim-Mak: Death-Point Striking
Dim Mak's 12 Most Deadly Katas: Points of No Return
The Encyclopedia of Dim-Mak: The Main Meridians
   (with Wally Simpson)
The Encyclopedia of Dim-Mak: The Extra Meridians, Points, and More
   (with Wally Simpson)
Power Taiji (with Michael Babin)
Secrets of Dim-Mak: An Instructional Video

Ultimate Dim-Mak: How to Fight a Grappler and Win

by Erle Montaigue

Copyright © 1996 by Erle Montaigue

ISBN 10: 0-87364-878-1
ISBN 13: 978-0-87364-878-3

Printed in the United States of America

Published by Paladin Press, a division of
Paladin Enterprises, Inc.
Gunbarrel Tech Center
7077 Winchester Circle
Boulder, Colorado 80301 USA
+1.303.443.7250

Direct inquiries and/or orders to the above address.

PALADIN, PALADIN PRESS, and the "horse head" design
are trademarks belonging to Paladin Enterprises and
registered in United States Patent and Trademark Office.

All rights reserved. Except for use in a review, no
portion of this book may be reproduced in any form
without the express written permission of the publisher.

Neither the author nor the publisher assumes
any responsibility for the use or misuse of
information contained in this book.

Visit our Web site at www.paladin-press.com

Contents

Foreword
vii

Preface
xiii

CHAPTER ONE
The Power
1

CHAPTER TWO
Abstract Antigrappler Training Methods
39

CHAPTER THREE
Fa-Jing Ch'uan Training Methods
117

Ultimate Dim-Mak: How to Fight a Grappler and Win

CHAPTER FOUR
The Mind of the Grappler
167

CHAPTER FIVE
Fighting Methods
175

CHAPTER SIX
The Sleeper Holds
205

Foreword

CORNERSTONES OF MONTAIGUE SELF-DEFENSE

Erle Montaigue is an Australian taiji practitioner whose mission is to teach taiji as originally intended—as a fighting art—rather than as only a healthful form of dance. While many agree with him, some so-called traditionalists view him as a renegade. Whatever the reader's orientation, Erle's views are bound to be stimulating.

One of Erle's favorite topics is self-defense, and why it's not at all unheard of for a so-called untrained street fighter to whip a black belt before he knows what's taking place. Having trained in conventional and unconventional martial arts, and having been a bouncer with a few street altercations to his name, Erle Montaigue brings a larger perspective to the question than many who have practiced a "sanitized" version of what used to be fighting arts.

When [Erle was] quizzed about what constitutes realistic training for a street encounter, it was soon apparent that [he] has developed a systematic approach that is based on both study with masters and his own experiences and research. What follows is a series of strong, interrelated beliefs about training and fighting that form the cornerstones of Montaigue self-defense.

1. Fight Instinctively

You cannot win a rough street encounter by following any kind of set pattern. Technique must be abandoned in the sense of planning out a set of moves. There is no time for contemplation or abstract reasoning. You must fight with whatever reflexes you have developed and trained. Winning or losing is often determined in the wink of an eye.

2. Use Your Reptilian Brain

The Chinese have a saying that a human being cannot fight. This means that one of the qualities separating mankind from so-called lower animals,the ability to reason abstractly, is a hindrance at the moment of battle.

To win in the street is to cease thinking as a human being and to fight instinctively, with the ferocity of a wild beast. Just as a snake may strike the part of a human that is closest to it, or some animals know instinctively to go for the throat, so must a person fight if he is to survive a brutal encounter.

The above statement is more than a metaphor. Science has now proven that we have not one brain but three brains that influence one another: the triune brain (see the *Triune Brain in Evolution,* by Paul McLean). The three brains (reptilian, limbic, and neo-cortex) are all active at the same time but to different degrees. The brain that houses the fight-or-flight response is the reptilian brain. It is this brain that can give us superhuman strength in time of need.

3. Develop Yang Energy

The reptilian brain makes use of extreme yang (hard, outgoing, aggressive, explosive) energy. This does not come naturally to many people because they have become too civilized. Montaigue has found that some people, especially certain women, find this very difficult to develop.

One exercise to develop a yang reaction to an attack is as follows. When the attacker makes his move, such as to lunge with both hands toward the throat of the defender, the defender throws both arms up, out, and with the fingers outstretched. This outstretching of the fingers seems to bring out the yang energy, which helps to activate the reptilian mind. Erle has found this to be the best way to help people who are timid by nature. Once the yang energy begins to flow, the defender can begin adding a blood-curdling scream. People often amaze themselves at the amount of power they can develop.

4. Fight Illogically

Street fighters do not fight logically. They know the value of surprise and unpredicability. If you try to fight systematically, such as using long-range techniques first, then mid-range, etc., the fight will be over before you realize what has happened.

Logical thinking may help a person avoid a fight in the first place, which is the ultimate victory, but the moment a battle starts there is no time for logical reasoning.

5. Use Eagle Vision

Although some instructors tell you to look the attacker in the eye, this works better in the training hall—and for dramatic effect in movies—than on the street. Such advice can even be dangerous, for a least two reasons. First, concentrating on someone's eyes is a sure way to practice tunnel vision. Not only does this make it difficult to see what that person's arms and legs are doing, but it is doubly difficult to be aware of the surroundings, including other possible

Ultimate Dim-Mak: How to Fight a Grappler and Win

attackers and physical objects that could impede your movement.

Secondly, if the other person has a more menacing glare than you—and attackers, by nature, usually do—you may lose confidence and therefore lose the confrontation right at that point.

Many animals, such as the eagle, are thought to mainly see the outline of objects rather than the minute details perceived by the human eye. Using eagle vision is nothing mystical. It is to be on wide-angle perception, to be aware of everything within your peripheral vision but to concentrate on nothing.

Peripheral vision has the potential for speeding up a person's reflexes. Theorists claim that peripheral vision provides a direct link to one's subconscious (Ostrander & Schroeder, *Super Memory: The Revolution, 1991*) Bypassing the conscious mind may provide for a faster response (Montaigue, "Using Peripheral Vision to Speed up the Reflexes,"*Australasian Fighting Arts Magazine, Dec./Jan. 1987.*) It could be compared to the fact that when a person touches something hot the nerve impulse goes to the spinal cord, which in turn sends the withdrawal signal to the arm. The brain learns about it after the fact. This accounts for why a person can react so quickly to a hot object.

Erle recommends the following exercise to help stimulate eagle vision. It should be practiced on both near and far objects, but for the beginner it would probably be best to choose an object at least a few feet away.

a. First, focus on an object so as to see detail (tunnel vision).

b. Second, without moving your eyes, try to become aware of everything within your range of vision. (Forget detail, as detail requires tunnel vision.)

c. Without moving the eyes, go back to the first step,

Foreword

then the second, etc. (Continue until you feel you need a rest. Don't overdo it.)

6. Forget Tournament Sparring (or Almost)

Probably the majority of instructors use some form of sparring as part of their teaching program. And it can have a place. Where Montaigue parts company with such instructors is when they believe that sparring approximates street defense. Erle contends that sparring is so far removed from street defense that it can be a hindrance rather than a help. And since Erle has had a few street confrontations, including facing knife attacks, he is speaking from experience.

Some believe that sparring can be a good exercise for building endurance (but most street fights only last seconds), developing a sense of distance, timing, balance (when on your feet), etc., but it is so far from real fighting that it can lead students into a false sense of security as far as truly being able to defend themselves on the street. In real battle, there are no rules. It's dirty, awkward, and ugly. And people usually end up fighting on the ground.

7. Protect the Safety of Your Training Partners

Since teaching taiji as a fighting art requires striking pressure points, and this is potentially lethal, Erle is adamant about protecting health during martial arts practice with a partner. Strikes to vulnerable areas should just be simulated or done very lightly.

Some instructors claim that many pressure point strikes, including knockouts, can be done safely. Erle did a number of knockouts also when he was less experienced. But one time he had great difficulty reviving a subject and so became much more conservative in his teaching demonstration approach.

For one thing, it's impossible to be completely knowledgeable about the health of the person you are striking.

There may be health problems that haven't yet surfaced, but which would render the person more sensitive to a particular technique.

Another consideration is that the more times a person has been knocked out, the more easily he can be knocked out the next time. There are numerous examples of this. And this is scary. What would this acquired weakness do to your chances of survival on the street? The answer is frighteningly clear.

The last question of the interview was to ask Erle if there was a shortage of barbers in Australia. With a laugh and a smile he answered no, and then went on to explain that his appearance is now much more subdued than in earlier years. At one time he was a rock music performer. The long hair is just a carryover from those days.

Actually, Erle is soft-spoken, mild-mannered, and rather conservative in many ways—quite different from what one might imagine from seeing him in pictures. But when it comes to self-defense, the wild man surfaces momentarily. And this is his advice to you.

—Arthur Smith
written for *Black Belt* magazine

Preface

At one time, such martial arts as kung fu and karate were considered the ultimate self-defense arts. During the Bruce Lee era, schools sprang up all over the world, and the martial arts were on the map, so to speak.

Now, martial artists are looking for something else. Somewhere along the way, the martial arts have lost their glory, their effectiveness. I think the reason is that too many martial arts teachers learned from books or learned only a tenth of a total system and then left that style or school to begin their own. And too many instructors who have either graded themselves up to black belt or had their students do so are awarding too many black belts too soon. They learn some movements and call it kung fu or karate. But kung fu and karate are much more than just movement, or how hard one can punch or kick. It takes years to learn a martial art properly, and to use it for self-defense takes even longer.

Most of the kick/punch martial arts have greatness, as do the grappling arts. The trouble nowadays is that the kick/punch arts have become so common, with so many offshoots, that they are losing their effectiveness, especially against grapplers (street fighters). The arts themselves have not lost effectiveness, but rather those who train in them have. We see people nowadays receiving black belts after one year! How is it possible to learn how to defend oneself in one year? I recently returned from the United States, where I discovered that it is possible to get a black belt from some organizations when you are able to perform the side splits! If people like Terry O'Neil (editor of *Fighting Arts International,* seventh dan, shotokan) had received his dan grading at the rate that they do nowadays, he would be 75th dan by now. (Sorry, Terry, giving your age away a bit there!) I know of many who are eighth dan but whose real rank should be brown belt! There is actually this old chap in the United States who is about 75 years of age, began training when he was 40, and now holds 75th dan!

The reason the martial arts take so long to learn properly is that we are not looking at just physical movement. Just about anyone can learn a kata or form, but what do they have? An empty book. Learning how to kick high and fast, punch hard and fast, and block is important but are only a small part of what we have to learn. It's the *internal* side that makes an ordinary martial art a great one. And this applies to kung fu as well as karate. Learning how to use a martial art for self-defense requires much more training, which comes in the form of "training methods" that cause unnatural movement to become natural movement and work at a reflex, or subconscious, level.

Because of the "demise" of the martial arts in general, other fighters, such as grapplers and wrestlers, jujutsu people, and so on, are beginning to make inroads into the martial arts' popularity. Some even put on tournaments—so-called "anything goes" events—and then invite so-called karate and kung fu people to fight against them. The grapplers win and claim that their style is superior. When Bruce Lee was around, and even before him, this was unheard of—kung fu and karate people actually knew how to punch and kick! And grapplers were used to test one's level of competence. Not so now, it would seem. And although we have the few older martial artists who have retained their initial greatness, the newer ones seem to have lost what was great.

Tournaments seem to have had an influence upon this, with many karate and kung fu people nowadays training only to win at tournaments and forgetting all about the fact that their art was originally intended for self-defense. Young martial artists make the big mistake of thinking that tournament fighting and self-defense attacks them, they lose. They just haven't done the groundwork. Some reach black belt standard in one year or even less, and they think they are unbeatable . . . until their first real street confrontation. Why? Because they have not yet learned how to turn their martial art into an art of self-defense.

Tournaments, one of my pet hates, are not real fighting, no matter how much they are promoted as being "anything goes," "full contact," and so on. In the United States there are now "Ultimate Fighting Championship" tournaments put on by an excellent family of jujutsu people, the Gracies. I would have to say that the Gracies are the best I have seen anywhere at what they do. They are excellent grapplers; they are stalkers. However, while these tournaments are supposed to be anything goes, there *are* rules. These include no biting, no groin shots, no eye gouges, and, I believe, no behind-the-neck shots. This, of course, leaves the front of the neck open, and a medium-powered attack to that area will kill someone. Thank God that not many of the combatants in these tournaments actually know how to fight! Otherwise we would have seen someone dead by now. It will probably happen, though, and then martial arts as a whole will be blamed. Governments will crack down on the martial arts once again, and we will all have to go into hiding just to practice our arts.

Ultimate Dim-Mak: How to Fight a Grappler and Win

These tournaments remind me of what the ancient Roman and, later, the Christian tournaments were like. They actually started as a kind of ceremony for burial, where two combatants would be hired to fight to the death, the dead one being buried with the corpse. The people wanted more and more blood, and hence the base spectacle of the Roman tournament where man was pitted against animal. Laws were passed so that wrongdoers could pay their debt to society by being fed to the lions, and so on. They eventually got out of hand, with bigger and better spectacles being produced to feed the public's need for blood. Interestingly enough, when the Roman empire fell and the Christians took over, the tournaments continued for another 200 years! Why? Because these tournaments were politically effective, with the politician who held the largest and most gruesome tournament invariably winning election!

Today, to a lesser degree, tournaments still feed that need for blood, that desire to see people hurt and on their knees. Why? Am I stupid or something? I regard tournaments as the most base of human activities, where one person must prove that he is better than the other by hurting him! The martial arts were invented so that we could defend ourselves and our families, not to hurt others for the sake of glory and blood lust.

The following is from the first part of an interview of Erle Montaigue conducted by Ron Baker of New York during Erle's U.S. and Canadian tours. Excerpts from the remainder of this interview will appear throughout the book.

ON ERLE'S EVOLVING PHILOSOPHY

I have had the opportunity in the past to travel with Erle Montaigue on his American workshop tour. So again, I took up the opportunity to travel with this wild man from down under.

Preface

I have known Erle for quite a number of years and have watched as he has grown and changed. These days, now that he is more at ease with us Americans, he is giving more out, and in some ways he is becoming harder in his own training. Erle Montaigue is an anomaly from the run-of-the-mill t'ai chi teacher. Many have expressed to me that he is more like a karate teacher, in that he pulls no punches and expects none to be pulled on him. Everything Erle says, he backs up with practical demonstration. When someone doesn't quite believe what Erle is saying, he simply asks him to attack full force, as this is the only way that some people will understand.

We Americans, too, are beginning to understand what this diverse teacher is all about. On the one hand he is a quiet, unassuming gentleman, but then when he begins to teach, the other side of Erle Montaigue—"the wild man of Oz"—comes right on through, electricity flying off in all directions as he demonstrates his unique ability in fa-jing, or explosive energy. Every sinew, muscle, and bone in his body explodes into unrestricted rage for a brief moment in time as he tries to get his point across—the point being that a person does not need huge muscles; strong, low stances; or amazing technical ability in order to defend himself.

I asked Erle a few questions again after his USA tour. As I look back on past articles I have written about Montaigue, I see the changes that have taken place in this man's life and way of teaching. He must be doing something right, as all of his American workshops were packed to capacity.

R: Erle, having seen you work in the past, I have noticed a great difference in the way that you teach now. You seem more at ease within yourself, and so you seem to make everyone else at ease. Everyone I spoke to remarked that as soon as they entered the training room, there was an atmosphere of calm-

ness. Are you doing something that we do not know about here?

E: Yes, I am feeling more at ease with my work nowadays. I must be truthful and say that in some ways I was not ready for all of the attention that I was receiving and wondered, why . . . me? Well, I think I'm beginning to find out the answers. I have always known that there was something bigger than just going around the world teaching people to fight! What am I giving to people? Nothing! In many ways I could not justify doing this for a living. Now, I am older, wiser, and I know that it is my job to help people to understand that we are all on this earth to help each other. And I believe that real martial artists, or warriors, can do a great deal of good for humankind simply by being there. I have noticed that whenever I give a class, there is a great amount of automatic healing going on, and people are actually healed simply by being there. And I now feel satisfied that I am doing something other than just teaching how to fight. I now use the martial arts as a way of simply meeting with and helping others to, in turn, help others.

I travel the world teaching huge groups of people, and I got to thinking, "Why?" The answer is to unite people all around the world in friendship and healing. This is already happening within my own organization, where we literally have friends in over 36 countries, all of whom can go to any of these countries and have a friend of like mind.

R: But what we learned at this workshop, the dim-mak and the small san-sau, really helped me in particular to understand my own karate; it really helped me to understand more about my own martial art.

E: What I teach has to be good, otherwise people would not come, and then there would be no reason for my own years of learning and teaching. Most people come for the "bad" stuff but soon realize that they cannot attain a high level only doing "the bad stuff." They must also know the "good" stuff, the healing side, in order to have a balance of yin and yang. It's the same with my videotapes. People usually begin with the "bad" ones, like the death-point striking, etc., but soon also realize that they must begin at the beginning. So most usually end up taking the earlier tapes on forms and healing as well.

R: Sounds like you have worked out your own philosophy on life. Are you religious? Are you a Taoist, for instance?

E: I was brought up in a small mining town south of Sydney, where things like Taoism and Buddhism were just foreign words. It's my belief that "what we were is what we are," so although I have studied most Eastern religions, I am still essentially a Christian. This doesn't mean that I go to church on a Saturday or Sunday or follow any particular religion. I like what Jesus has to say and try to follow this as best I can, although it isn't easy. Lao Tze and Buddha said much the same things as Jesus anyway.

R: So how do you justify being a Christian and doing the martial arts?

E: I am always asked this question. As I have said, I believe that it is impossible to be like Jesus Christ. He was a man among men, whom I believe to be the strongest man to ever live. I justify doing the martial arts not only for the healing reasons, but also because of the biblical saying, "He who helps himself will be helped [by God?]." So, if I am attacked, I shouldn't just stand there and expect God to help me, because I am not helping myself. Nor should I just stand there as someone else is attacked, because I am not helping him to begin with. If I defend myself, I am helping myself; then God will help in making my martial art the very best that it can be. Turning the other cheek is okay when it is insults or bad talk about you. This is hard enough to do, but why die because you wish not to defend yourself? I'm sure Christ would not wish that to happen, so in cases where life is

threatened, or where someone else who is weaker than the attacker is attacked, sure, we help.
R: So, do you mind if I ask you about the martial arts?
E: Of course not. I'm not a priest! The martial arts are the physical things that cause internal things to change in people, so it is very important that I do my own thing, using the martial arts.

With this book I have tried to give something great back to kung fu and karate: a way of dealing with a good grappler simply by using what we have and what we have learned in a realistic manner. Many of the things that I talk about may seem quite basic to some, like how to punch. But it's amazing just how many so-called highly ranked black belts simply don't know how to punch. They are wonderful at kata and win their tournaments of noncontact. But most only have a couple of lessons on punching because it is assumed that everyone knows how to punch. So they have these few lessons from someone who also does not know how to punch, and then they get onto what they think is the "real" stuff, the kumite! I'm not saying that *all* schools are like this; however, an increasing number of new schools are. And it's a sad sign of the times that the simpler the methods of the school, the more students they have. If it's even a little difficult, then people do not wish to put in the time necessary to learn properly. They want "results" from their first class.

It takes many years to gain the fa-jing power necessary to make the body move in a way that will make your punches devastating without even drawing your fist back. And it takes much effort to be able to attack in defense in a split second with much power and speed. Many lose speed when they try to punch hard or power when they try to punch fast. In kung fu and karate, we do not punch fast—we explode! And anything that the fist touches is gone. I have seen so-called highly ranked black belts and so-called world champions punch a jujutsu person, for instance, in the face, and nothing happened! Why? Because first, that person is not a karateka or a kung fu person, really, and second, he does not know how to punch; he does not know how to get the power, and he does not know where to strike.

If you only read one chapter in this book, it should be the one on training methods. Training methods are the most important tools of any martial artist who wishes to turn his art into self-defense. Do not think that because you know a few katas and have won at kumite several times you know about self-defense. Self-defense is an instinctive, animalistic way of fighting, and this is only learned through training methods.

These training methods teach you how to internalize what you have learned physically into the subconscious mind, so that when you are attacked in the street you do not take a stance, nor do you think about what technique you will use. You do not use technique as such—you just hit your attacker! In taiji we call this kind of internal, subconscious, reflexive response "nontechnique." If you have only trained in kata and kumite in the dojo, technique is what you will do in a really dangerous situation, and you will lose—perhaps your life. Fights do not happen logically; kata and kumite are logical, and the two can never mix.

It is the training methods that turn our logical martial art into an illogical way of fighting. Once you have this, you are able to confuse an attacker because you do not react logically to his attacks.

When fighting against other styles of the kick/punch variety, grapplers will use completely illogical methods.

Or rather, you perceive them to be illogical. The grappler's methods are actually quite logical for his style of fighting, but they seem illogical to you. If you try to fight against a grappler using karate or kung fu "techniques," as such, he will beat you. If, however, you have done the training methods inherent in all great martial arts systems, then you will not be beaten because you will be fighting illogically to his logical way of fighting. You will be doing things that he will not expect you to do. Thus, his "internal switches" will not be turned on, and he will be confused.

How can you expect to fight anyone, let alone a grappler, having learned only kata and kumite? You are still the same person you were before you took up the martial arts; nothing has changed. You might as well take up track and field! You need something more than just movement if you wish to learn self-defense. You need a way of turning yourself into someone or something else, like an animal. You need to change your whole attitude toward fighting.

Your instructor needs to tell you the truth, that what you learn in your first four years does not give you self-defense but only the groundwork upon which to lay the self-defense training. When you have learned the katas and are confident at kumite, *then* you begin to learn self-defense. It is my belief that any grading should not be given until the person has learned all of the groundwork. And a black belt should not be given until the instructor is assured that the student is able to defend himself in the street. Only in this way will the martial arts regain their former glory.

The longest chapter in this book covers training methods, not techniques. However, you will find that within these methods are all of the techniques that you will need to defend yourself against anyone or any style. But you will gain these techniques internally and not actually learn them as techniques per se. If you get through the chapter on training methods and have a partner with whom to train, you will find that your level of competence in using the martial arts as a self-defense tool will increase to a very high level.

CHAPTER

The Power

ONE

In discussing "the power," it is necessary to talk about fa-jing, which is the groundwork needed to gain the power to fight any grappler. Later, I will be talking about techniques to use against a grappler, but technique without the power is like a Rolls-Royce without an engine.

You do not have to be superfit nor super strong to have real power. If you have a working body you have all the power you need to defeat a good grappler or any assailant. Nowadays we see body builders, runners, and athletes being heralded as the new, super martial artists. They have muscles coming out of their ears and look superfit. But this has nothing to do with the martial arts and self-defense. If martial artists have to have "Atlas" bodies, then the founders of the martial arts systems must have got it wrong. We must, however, be healthy—and health and fitness are not the same. I have seen so many so-called superfit human beings die of heart attack from ill health. You can be healthy and not fit, or you can be fit and unhealthy. Better to be fit *and* healthy.

A person who knows the martial arts is able to defend him/herself without being superfit or superstrong. The way we do this is to use the whole body rather than just the peripherals and to know where to strike to end a confrontation in seconds.

Martial arts are not sports. People have tried to make sports out of the martial arts, but it's a bit like trying to make poisoning someone into a sport! You would use sugar instead of arsenic, and the only thing you'd learn is how to put the sugar into the glass. It cannot be done—you completely ruin the original self-defense art by making it into a sport. You cannot become an animal, maiming and killing, in the ring. And that's what the martial arts is all about—survival, not sports.

When I talk about "power," I mean total power, and this means speed as well. I don't particularly mean huge muscular power, pumping iron, and so on. The "power" means internal power, making use of the whole body and not just one part, such as the fist. The power comes from the way we move the body, rather than just pushing out a fist. I have seen fighters down their opponents and then punch them fully in the face and head, with hardly any effect. If they knew how to punch, the fight would be over, with one person dead! Perhaps that's a good way of stopping these potentially dangerous so-called anything-goes fights.

The body is the most important part in gaining the power. How you move the body will deter-

Figure 1

The Power

3

mine whether you can knock someone out with your first punch or have him continue to rush at you and take you down. I'll cover exactly where to punch later, but for now, we gain the power.

The body must be totally relaxed, arms loose, and hands open and loose. You stand with one foot slightly forward of the other, the same for the hands (fig. 1). If you were to move your waist quickly, the arms and hands would also shake, because they are loose and connected to the body. When your hands are stiff, so too are your arms, and they will not move freely when your waist moves.

ON GAINING "THE POWER"

R: I know you distinguish between your workshops and those of some others, where there is more talk than doing. You promised us work and work we did! But many here were finding the going tough as this movement is so different to what we in the karate field are used to. From all the talk between the attendees, they all can see the power that can be generated and are all trying to "get it." I mean, we look at you doing that explosive movement, but it isn't easy to get it.

E: It doesn't matter what style you are practicing; you are doing the groundwork for reflex actions to begin. The reason that some found it difficult has to do with their level of competence in their own martial art to begin with. Some, who are only at the beginning of their training found it somewhat easier than those who have been training in unnatural movements for 25 years! Others who have been training in a somewhat better style of karate found the going not so difficult and with some effort were able to gain a great amount of power over short distances in a relatively shorter period. These training methods will help to make your karate what it should be. I'll tell you the same story that I always tell at these times. Sensei Chitose, when he was alive, was the founder of Chito-ryu Okinawan karate. He would come to Australia and teach the normal karate way of moving—stiff and muscularly powerful. However, whenever he demonstrated, his students observed that he was like a rubber man; his body would shake, and it was as if he was a rag doll. He would say that this was the highest way of doing karate, like taiji!

So I believe that there is something more than just the stiff physical movement side of karate, but they just aren't telling, or many of the modern sensei just don't know. You see, it doesn't matter how intelligent you are, how many books you have read, how much research you have done, or how many acupuncture exams you have taken if you simply can't do it! It must be your body that learns and not your conscious mind. And your body will not experience this way of moving if all you ever do is static, stiff kata.

R: Many from our field (karate) say that they are not moving stiffly, they do shake.

E: Yes, they shake relatively so, as opposed to someone who is totally stiff, but this shaking is still controlled. It is not totally out of control, which is what reflex actions are. At the point of impact, the body is totally out of control for that split second, and this is what many karateka cannot understand because the Japanese way in particular is so ordered, so controlled. If you have the chance to look at someone like, for instance, Sensei Keiji Tomiyama when he performs his upper level katas,[you'll see that] he does them very unkarate-like, again like a rubber man. There are still karateka out there who almost give themselves hernias when they perform their sanchin kata—the neck muscles stick out, as do the blood vessels. This is not good for health or the martial arts. There is an old saying from karate, you must not hear the sound (of the breathing).

The Power

5

When you know how to punch, then you will have "the power," as real punching cannot be done without "the power."

Your waist must move first. If I were to show you how to punch slowly, you would not see the waist move first, both upper body and lower body would move simultaneously. However, when I move in a fa-jing way, explosively, the waist must move so fast that it leaves the upper body behind for that split second. When the upper body finally catches up with the waist and hips, tremendous power is generated. It's like pulling a piece of elastic that has a stone connected to one end, as opposed to having a piece of string. When you pull the string, the rock moves at the same pace as the string, but when you pull the elastic quickly, there is a time when the elastic is loading, and then when there is enough power to pull the rock, all of that built up potential energy explodes into the rock, causing it to move forward with great speed and power. It is the same when we move the waist explosively. But this can only happen when there is looseness in the whole body.

I have many karate people studying with me, and in the beginning they all, bar none, say that they use this method of turning the waist. But they soon find that it is not the same, they are *trying* to turn the waist, and this causes tension and stiffness. If the body is stiff, then the upper body will try and move when the waist moves, losing any real power. But if the body is loose, and the waist moves suddenly, the upper body, arms, and fists will move a little after the waist and have all of that potential energy to release when it strikes.

Many instructors tell me that they do move the waist; however, upon closer inspection, we see that this is a controlled turning, with the practitioner actually turning the waist himself, and not allowing the movement or what it is he is doing to actually cause the waist to move. So, it becomes a stiff muscular movement with

Ultimate Dim-Mak: How to Fight a Grappler and Win

6

Figure 2

Figure 3

any rebound snuffed out by the body stiffness. This leaves no room to reattack if necessary. This stiff kind of turning of the waist makes for a nice crisp "crack" when the gi (karate training outfit) snaps upon impact but has little real power.

I will punch the mitt using a "normal" punch (that which is perceived to be normal by most karate standards), as in Figure 2. The mitt is pushed and not struck as such. It would cause some damage in many cases, but when there is a raving lunatic at the other end, then this kind of punch perhaps would not stop him, because you have only damaged that portion of his body that you struck. We need to be able to strike someone and do great damage to the whole body and the internal energy system or nervous system.

Figure 3 shows the same strike, but this time I am using fa-jing. Now there has been a loud "cracking" sound as the fist strikes the mitt. The

The Power

mitt moves away violently, and I have used the rebound from that fa-jing movement to recover and be ready, "cocked," or sprung, like a wound-up spring, ready to explode again (fig. 4).

LOOSENING THE WAIST

Fa-jing punching cannot be done without a loose waist. An exercise first to see if your waist is loose, and also to help it to loosen, is as follows.

Your partner stands opposite you. You are standing with both feet parallel, about shoulder width apart. You are trying to hold your hips pointing toward the front, while your partner will be turning your shoulders (waist), as in Figure 5.

Your partner now begins to turn your shoulders to his right, pushing with his left hand and pulling with his right. You must keep your hips to the front while allowing him to turn your waist. This may sound easy. However, you will find that you will be helping him to

Figure 4

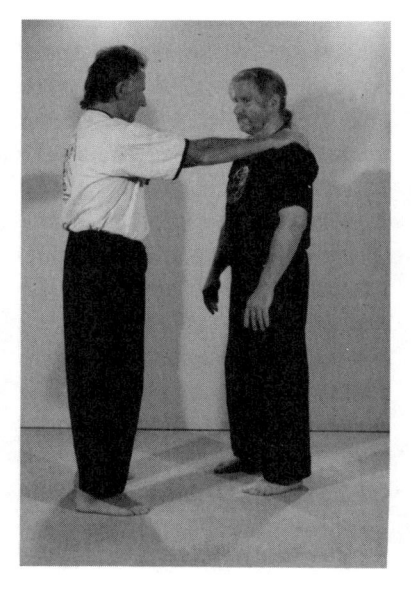

Figure 5

Figure 6

Figure 7

turn your waist by turning it yourself. This is not relaxed. Or you will be trying to hold your waist using muscular power. Both are wrong. You must simply relax your waist and allow your partner to turn you—not helping, not resisting. Your partner will feel some resistance, in fact quite a lot, but will be able to tell if you are providing that resistance by physically pushing against him. He or she will also be able to tell if you are assisting, as the turning will be too easy (fig. 6). Here is the test. Your partner lets go of your shoulders and moves out of the way quickly to avoid being struck by your swinging hands. If there is a slight delay before your waist moves, or if your waist moves back slowly, then you are not relaxed. If your waist moves back instantly with power, and shuffles to the front, left, right, left, right, etc., then you are loose.

POWER PUNCHING

Now that your waist is loose, we can begin learn-

The Power

9

ing how to punch by using that power gained from the waist. Most people will find it difficult to turn the waist in the opposite direction that they would normally turn to punch. For instance, most people will turn the waist to the left to throw a right-handed punch (fig. 7). What I am telling you is to turn your waist to the right to throw a right-handed punch! It's not as difficult as it seems.

Remember that what you are reading and seeing now happens at an explosive pace. Standing as in Figure 8, you begin to turn your waist to your left, keeping in mind that the waist will be moving slightly ahead of the shoulders and hence the hands (fig. 9). Your waist moves further to the left, which causes your right hand to begin to move outward (fig. 10). When you began, your right palm faced downward; now it is turning over to face up. As your palm catches up with your waist, it turns over and

Figure 8

Figure 9

closes into a fist (fig. 11). But because the waist was ahead of the fist, it has turned back to the right just as the fist makes contact (fig. 12). Figure 13 shows the correct fist with the thumb flush with the third knuckle of the forefinger. When we use this type of fist, it is said to bring "yin and yang" right into the palm, giving greater power. It will feel difficult at first, because you are probably used to holding the more "normal" fist where the thumb is clenched around the fingers. This type of fist only creates external tension.

Figure 10

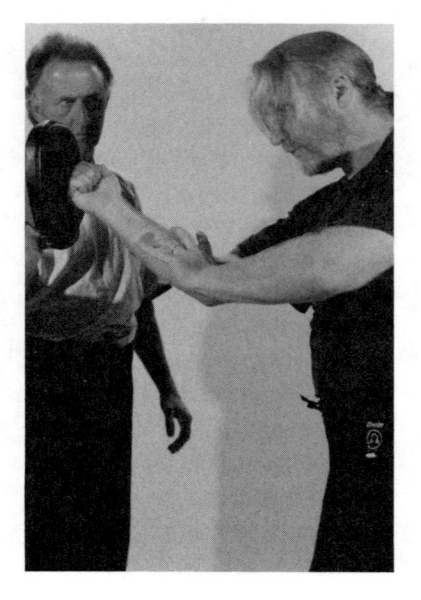

Figure 11

The Power

11

Figure 12

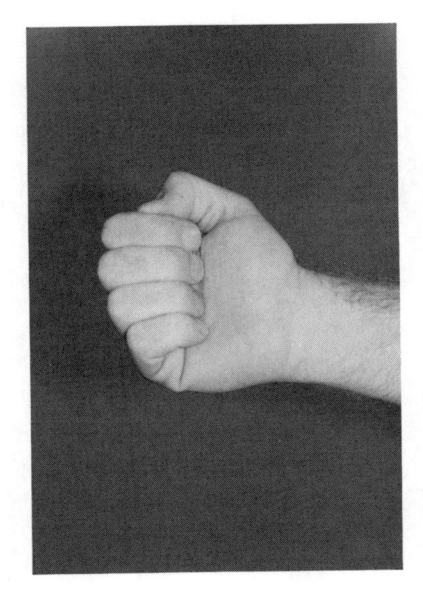

Figure 13

Ultimate Dim-Mak: How to Fight a Grappler and Win

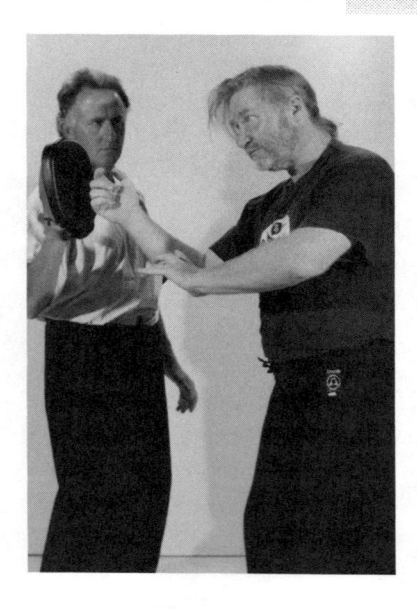

12

Figure 14

Figure 15

As soon as the fist makes contact, it is released and becomes a palm again, as in Figure 14.

The waist has moved to the left violently, which causes the palm to be thrust outward, but as the palm snaps into a fist and strikes, the waist has already turned back to the right, causing a snapping action on the fist, a bit like the end of a whip. Notice too that the left heel has come off the ground and has turned inward (fig. 15). The heel is not pulled off the ground by you; it just comes off the ground because of the action of the body in performing fa-jing. So do not *try* to turn the heel; just move the body so explosively that the heel will move. You will also notice what the left palm is doing. I have not physically raised it, but rather the movement has caused the rebound to make the hand rise, ready to strike. I have utilized the rebound from this fa-jing movement to cause another attacking move to happen subconsciously.

The Power

13

You will see in later chapters that we fight a grappler by not stopping once we have begun. Each fa-jing attack causes another one to happen until the grappler is downed.

THE VOICE

The voice is the mediator between physical movement and abstract thought. So if we are able to make a "fa-jing" sound with the movement, it will help greatly in learning about fa-jing. The sound should not be a long sound like "har," but a cracking or popping sound like "pah." The sound should happen at the precise moment of impact (fig. 16). I know you cannot hear the sound, but you can "see" the sound from what the body is doing in the photo.

Begin with your fingers touching the mitt (fig. 17). Try to punch the mitt with as much power as possible, doing the above-waist movements, without bringing your palm back. This will feel "pissy" (Australian slang for weak) at first, but

Figure 16

Figure 17

with practice you will be able to attack the mitt with great power even from this short distance (fig. 18).

The area of impact is the last three knuckles, not the forefinger knuckle (fig. 19). You will notice some soreness around the area of the small fingers, but do not wear gloves of any kind; we do not defend ourselves wearing gloves! I have seen many so-called full-contact fights where the combatants have to stop because their hands have become so sore from hitting real objects. So we develop our hands by hitting things without gloves. If they do become red and sore, or even bleed, pack the sore area in ice to relieve it. I remember having bleeding spaces between my knuckles, and it would feel like heaven to put the back of my palm down in the freezer.

Everything I show in this book comes from realistic experience, and many of the training methods come from times when one of my students just couldn't get something

Figure 18

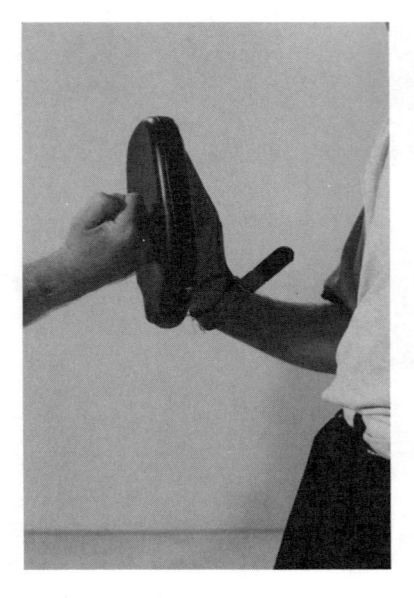

Figure 19

The Power

15

and I had to work out a way of teaching him or her how to do it. One such way came when one of my students just could not get the turning over of the palm upon impact—he kept wanting to punch with the palm facing down, as is taught in most karate schools. I simply told him to hold his palm facing down (fig. 20), and then, as quickly as he could, snap the palm over to face up, closing the fist as he did this (fig. 21). If you don't hear a sound when the fingers make a fist, the movement was not fa-jing.

Figure 20

Next we go back to the mitt. You must now punch the mitt using that same method of turning the palm over violently to make a sound; the only difference is that you are now allowing the waist to force your fist outward in a circle.

Upon impact, the fist does not just stop; it will continue its natural curve back to your left-hand side (or right side if using your left fist). You control it so that it does not go back too

Figure 21

far, thus making it useless for reattacking (fig. 22). The curve for this fist is a counterclockwise one. The knuckles do not "slide" on the mitt, because the mitt moves away the instant the fist hits it. If I were to allow the wrist to continue on its path, it would go past my left hip (fig. 23) and back to my right-hand side.

Do not look down! Many students make the mistake of looking down upon impact; this causes you to lose power and puts you at a disadvantage as far as any reattack is concerned, and it also leaves you open to attack (fig. 24). The head should be held as if suspended from above by a piece of string. It should be as if there is a piece of pipe stuck up your spine preventing it from bending at the neck. The reason? Fa-jing is centrifugal; real power is centrifugal.

If you hold a straight piece of pipe, for instance, with a cross-member at the top, then twist the pipe at the shaft, the cross-member will spin freely with

Figure 22

Figure 23

The Power

17

power. If, however, that pipe is bent, all of that centrifugal power will be lost at the bend, and the cross-member will not spin freely with any power.

This is what we have to do with the body. And this is why we do not take huge "kung-fu" type stances. The less distance you have between your feet (within reason, of course; you must stand there with balance), the more centrifugal power you can generate by using the whole body. If you have a very large stance, as in Figure 25, then the power will only come from your arms and legs, with no help from the waist.

The classics say that the power comes from the "bubbling well" point (Kidney 1 or K 1, as shown in fig. 26) at the base of the foot, up through the legs, and is directed by the waist, manifesting in the hands. If we have a low stance, this power is lost in holding us up; it does not come through the waist to manifest in the hands. The power originates in the

Figure 24

Figure 25

legs but is not powered by the legs. The waist causes the power to be magnified greatly. Like a small stone being thrown into a fan, the initial force does not have to be great—you just lob the stone—but when it hits the fan, the force multiplies as it is propelled outward.

Although I have shown how the body moves in photos, it is almost impossible to show the fa-jing fully. When I punch the mitt, I can show you what the waist, the feet and hands, etc., do. But the absolute explosiveness must be seen and felt. At the precise moment of impact, even the feet are not on the ground. The force generated by the whole body is so great that the feet actually leave the ground for that split second (fig. 27), not as a result of my actually doing it, but as a result of the explosive movement of which I have no control for that moment. Like a sneeze, I am in control just before and just afterward, but totally out of control as it is happening. (So many car accidents have happened as a direct result of a sneeze!)

The waist is the most difficult aspect of this fa-jing

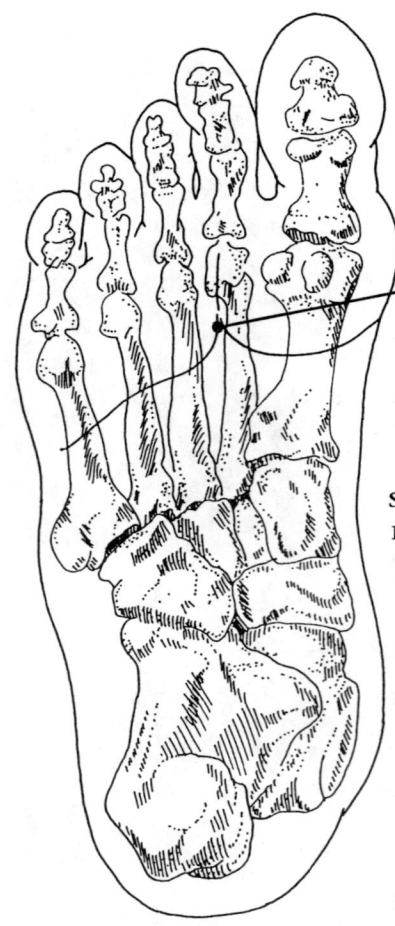

Figure 26

The Power

19

punch to learn. But if you can learn how to do it, then the whole of fa-jing and the power that comes with it will be yours. To this end, I have worked on a couple of training methods with my students to gain this somewhat awkward method of moving the waist. (Actually, it is only awkward when it is *not* done not as a fa-jing movement, but it is essential and relatively easy when done as a fa-jing movement.)

Stand with your palm outstretched just forward of the mitt. In Figure 28 you turn your waist to your left to indicate the initial turning of the waist just before the turn back to the right. Next you turn your right palm up and close your fist as you attack the mitt. As you do this, and to gain some power, you turn your waist back to your right (fig. 29). This will teach you how to turn your waist in the correct direction upon impact.

Another method is to strike the mitt, using the correct turning of the waist to your left (opposite

Figure 27

Figure 28

Ultimate Dim-Mak: How to Fight a Grappler and Win

if striking with the left fist), and as the fist makes contact, to turn your waist to your right to strike your partner's left shoulder with your left hand (fig. 30). This will cause you to have to turn your waist back to your right in order to strike his shoulder.

Figure 29

Figure 30

The Power

21

OTHER WEAPONS

The same principle applies to all of the other weapons that we will be using against a grappler. The open palm is also used in exactly the same way, gaining its momentum and power from the whole body, initiated by the legs and powered by the waist. I am standing in front of the mitt, with my right palm "loaded yang." The palm is limp in a yin shape, so therefore is loaded with yang energy. Turning the waist to the left violently, I leave my left palm behind momentarily (fig. 31). As it catches up with this momentum, and as the waist explodes back to my right, the palm explodes outward, releasing the yang energy (fig. 32). This is the same principle as with the fist.

Figure 31

Figure 32

Figure 33

Figure 34

The elbow is the same. I turn my waist so quickly to my left (or right if doing it on the other side) that my right elbow is left behind, as in Figure 33. As my waist turns back to my right, the elbow is slammed into the target (fig. 34). The power generated by the waist and the whole body is the most power that any individual is able to generate. You are not relying upon the size of your triceps or your biceps; this is now irrelevant, because you are using the total power of your whole body. Even a smaller person is able to generate great power using the whole body. Every part of the body will be used. In fact, when we say that the whole body is a weapon, we don't mean that the elbow is a weapon, the shoulder is a weapon, the head is a weapon, and so on. The *whole body* is actually a weapon. Which brings me to the next part of the power training.

THE FA-JING SHAKE

In any fighting situation in which a grappler is

The Power

23

one of the combatants, don't look at the grappler; look at what the other person is doing. Basically, he is just standing there trying to do back to the grappler what the grappler is doing to him. And this is playing right into the grappler's hands. He wants you to try and grapple with him; that's what he is best at. And it's a funny human phenomenon that when we are touched by another person, we try to emulate what that person is doing to us. Hence, we will see kickboxers, karateka, and savate people trying to out-grapple a grappler, never thinking to punch or kick. The person who does this will lose every time because he is relying on the physical strength of his arms or legs or neck, not his whole body.

This next exercise is useful for two scenarios. The first is when the attacker has not yet made contact but is coming in, and the second is when the grappler finally grabs you. If, however, you are grabbed by the grappler, then you have not read this book very well, because being grabbed is what we try to avoid at all costs. (I'll be covering avoidance methods later in this book.)

You simply have your partner grab you either from the front or back (figs. 35 and 36). He holds you fairly tightly, but not so tightly that you cannot move. (Later when you are able to make use of true fa-jing, it will not matter how tightly he holds you. But in order to get a grasp on this exercise, he holds you moderately tight.)

Figure 35

Ultimate Dim-Mak: How to Fight a Grappler and Win

You shake violently—a fa-jing shake with the whole body as if you have just done the punching mentioned earlier in this chapter. If your partner does not feel any kind of shock, which would cause him to either let you go or release his grip sufficiently for you to counter, then you have not used a fa-jing movement. If, however, you are able to shock him causing him to let go, then you are getting there (fig. 37).

Figure 36

Figure 37

The Power

25

You have simply shaken your whole body violently from side to side, not just turning so that he is able to follow or stop you, but violently so that he is also shaken violently. With your first shake he tries to move to one side, but now your waist shakes back the other way, causing him to be shocked. If used in a realistic situation and during training, you would of course use one or more of your peripheral weapons like your elbows (figs. 38 and 39).

Figure 38

THE WAIST POWER

In order to gain great "internal" waist power, we use a method that I learned from my amateur and pro wrestling days—the old "referee's hold." I like to use this method, as it far outstrips any weight-training method in terms of effectiveness for self-defense. We fight against humans, so we train with humans and not dead weights.

The idea of using the referee's hold is not for competition, but rather so that two bodies will be

Figure 39

Ultimate Dim-Mak: How to Fight a Grappler and Win

locked onto each other so that one is unable to move without the other moving.

An old wrestler once taught me that you must never play the opponent's game, and I used to win my share of matches by adhering to that advice. When we used to go into the referee's hold, I would not push and shove as my opponent attempted, but rather I would try to neutralize his power by doing the exact opposite and yielding my other side. If he attacked on my right side, I would turn my waist slightly to my left and vice versa. This would neutralize his attacks and thus wear him down more quickly. When the time was right, I would find an opening and throw him to the canvas. This, of course, has nothing at all to do with real fighting; I only introduce it here as a part of this next training method.

Your partner grasps you around your neck with his left hand, and you take the back of his neck with your left hand. Each of you is holding tightly onto each other's elbows with your

Figure 40

Figure 41

right palms, and your heads are touching (fig. 40). The object is to try to throw each other off balance by turning your waists. Do not push and shove; we are training the waist only. Of course, the whole body gets a great physical workout because this is very strenuous. Try to stay centered as you turn your waist, not allowing your partner to get the upper hand. Sink down into your lower abdomen physically as well as mentally, push your mind down low into your stomach, and then start working your waist in attack as well as in defense (fig. 41).

The above exercise will help to generate real power in your waist, which will in turn help to generate real fa-jing power throughout the whole body.

CONNECTIVITY

Connectivity is part of your total power, without which your arms, legs, hands, and head would all work independently. We want the whole body to work as a unit: when one part moves, so too does the whole.

The first connection is between the hands and the waist. If the waist moves and the hands do not, then you do not have fa-jing. Most Western people move like this, relying on the most obvious muscles to do their work. For instance, when someone is picking something up from the floor, he will bend down (wrong), grab it with his hand, bend up (wrong), and then use

Figure 42

only the biceps to "curl" the object upward. In order to use the whole body connectively, using this example, one must squat (fig. 42), pick the object up, and then stand up using the legs, keeping the back straight and the chin pulled in. Here I have used my whole body to pick up the object (fig. 43). Just on a health level, many people sustain long-term lower back problems from simply putting things into the trunk of their cars. Rather than

Figure 43

Figure 44

The Power

holding something heavy and reaching inside of the trunk to put it down (fig. 44), you should place one foot into the trunk first, and then, using your whole body, place the object down (fig. 45).

We have an exercise to teach us connectivity from taijiquan (t'ai chi). It comes from our "push hands" exercises. These exercises are to teach us tactile sense—touching another person and knowing what he or she is going to do. It involves two people using four different techniques to push and pull each other and to counter those pushes and pulls. That's it in a nutshell. Your partner stands opposite you. He is told to resist slightly to your power. You place your palm onto his shoulder (fig. 46). Now, you turn your waist to your left. The very instant that your waist turns, so too should the power increase on his shoulder (fig. 47). In other words, your right palm is pushing him to your left as your waist turns. If

Figure 45

Figure 46

there is no push or buildup of power on his shoulder, then your waist and arm are not connected. You have left your arm behind. Even a fleeting break between when your waist moves and when your arm moves is wrong. Concentrate upon your waist and your lower back area; there is a tremendous amount of power in that region that we never really use, or at least are unaware that we use, especially on a lateral level. Pull your chin in and think about your waist muscles. Only use the waist to try to move your partner. Do not use your shoulder, as in Figure 48. See how the palm has moved from my center; my waist has turned to my left, but my right palm has stayed where it is and has tried to use shoulder power to push forward. I have not used lateral or centrifugal power.

You may feel some soreness around the lower back and waist area after doing this exercise, but it is it only good old muscu-

Figure 47

Figure 48

lar pain from not using that part of your body for so long. Your partner will be able to tell you when it is happening incorrectly. Maybe you won't even notice when you are doing it incorrectly.

QIGONG FOR GAINING INTERNAL HEALTH

By doing all of the above, you will gain a certain amount of extra power, and you will feel it immediately. However, this may not be true internal power unless the fa-jing is real and not gained from just the body being loose. You will feel power from the body simply being loose, but when you finally have absolute coordination and connectivity, grounding, and a free qi flow, then you will feel real internal power.

To gain this internal power more easily, we should do the following qigong exercises. These exercises expedite what we have to do to gain internal power and enable us to have the power of the ground.

The power of the ground, or as my old mate Mike (Iron Mike) Sigman calls it, "p'eng strength," does not simply mean that we push off the ground to gain power using the strength of our legs. It means that we actually use the power from the ground, or "earth qi" (mother qi). Let me explain.

Everything that is talked about in the internal arts, that which was left to us by the masters of old, pertains to the ground. We are not told to be "aired"! We are told to be grounded. The forms, the qigongs, and the grounding exercises are to help us gain and use ground qi. Everything on this earth is in some way attached to the ground by roots. A tree is an obvious example here. Its physical roots go deep into the earth to gain this ground qi. But all animals have roots too, which go deep into the earth. These roots are energy roots. We human beings somewhat limit our roots by simply being human. Tension, bad living habits, and so on cause us to lose some of our roots.

Through these energy roots we are able to make use of the ground qi to gain internal power.

So the qigongs help us to gain our roots again, or to repair them. Only then can we gain internal power. The power (qi) coming through our roots into the earth (mother) activates, strengthens, and gives us a normal amount of qi. This activation and growth of our own qi then allow us to use the energy of the ground to literally direct the ground energy through our bodies.

This flow of ground qi can be used in a number of ways—to heal someone else, to heal the earth, or to defend ourselves against disease or external attack. It can never be used to harm another person, animal, or plant. Only if your own life or that of someone else is threatened can you make use of the earth qi for self-defense manner.

If you look at most native peoples, you will see that they, through their dances or daily movement, all have a way of grounding and growing their energy roots. The Africans have their dance, and it is not like Western dance, which is generally "up"—the energy is up into the chest and head, and we generally try to have a light, elevated, "beautiful" appearance, as in ballet. This way of dance is adverse to grounding. Native peoples try to pound themselves into the ground when they dance, with the main emphasis on the feet and legs. One "grounding" dance from Africa simply has the practitioners jumping up and sinking their heels into the

Figure 49

earth. As they do this, their entire bodies rise and fall into the earth via the heels (fig. 49 and 50). Native Americans also use dance to gain the ground qi, as do the Australian Aborigines. When I had the opportunity to talk with Aboriginal elders here in Australia, I was amazed at the correlation between their beliefs about energy and what I have learned. When an Aborigine dances, you can literally see the ground flying up all around him because he stomps his feet so hard into the ground. The Chinese also know about this, hence the grounding qigongs, which have also been handed down from generation to generation.

The heels are very important in grounding. In pushing the heels down into the ground, we activate the "qi entering" point called Kidney 1. This point is where the ground qi comes into the body, and it is the heels that activate it. So, when we sink into the ground through the heels, we do not think about K1

Figure 50

Figure 51

Ultimate Dim-Mak: How to Fight a Grappler and Win

Figure 52

Figure 53

point, but rather we simply push the heels into the ground by placing all of the body weight on them.

Stand as in Figure 51. Place your weight on the rear foot, in this case the right heel. This activates K1 to receive ground qi. Hold your left hand vertically with fingers pointing out so that the left elbow is over the left knee. Hold the right palm facing down. Here is the important part: pretend your arms are branches on a tree, just hanging there, and sink your energy into the ground via your heel. Place your tongue on the hard palate, and breathe through your nose.

Push with your left foot so that your waist turns slightly to your left (fig. 52). As you do this, imagine that you are breathing in through your right palm at the Laogong point, or Pericardium 8. You are thinking breathing in at this point. Now push all of your weight back onto your right heel. As you exhale, push your weight lightly onto the left foot (heel), and turn your waist slightly to your right. Imagine that you are breathing out through your left fingertips (fig. 53). With the last bit of exhalation, you return to the beginning posture and begin again. Do this 10 times, and then change legs and do it 10 times on the reverse side.

The next "power" qigong begins in the same stance with your left foot forward and your arms placed by your sides (fig. 54). As you turn your waist to your left, open your arms outward and breathe in slowly and deeply. A little weight moves onto your left (front) foot (fig. 55). As you turn your waist back to your right, exhale and sit back on your rear foot as your arms move in front of you and push down (fig. 56). Inhale through your nose, with your tongue placed on your hard palate. Exhale through your mouth, with your tongue placed on your lower palate. Do this 10 times, and then reverse the stance.

Figure 54

Figure 55

Figure 56

Figure 57

Both of the above qigongs can be done on any surface; however, all of these power exercises are enhanced if they are done out in the open near some trees while standing on grass. The next qigong must be done on grass in the open, preferably on a mountaintop or in the country, where some fresh air can be found.

With a right-foot-forward stance, turn your waist a little to your left and sit back on your rear leg. As you do this, both of your arms move out. The right one circles clockwise, while the left moves counterclockwise (fig. 57). Your waist will turn back to the right as you finally sit back fully on your rear leg. Your palms do tight circles and scoop inward (figs. 58 and 59). As you sit back fully, both palms now poke straight up while facing toward you (fig. 60). This whole movement only takes a very short time, and you are inhaling all the while.

Once you are fully weighted back and your

The Power

37

palms are higher than your face, turn them down (fig. 61). As you exhale quickly, your palms push down so hard that it causes both feet to be pushed into the ground at the heels. The feet may even be lifted off the ground momentarily just before the push (fig. 62). Do this only three times on each side in the morning.

The above will give you the necessary power to deal with any attack, but the power training does not end here. All of the exercises given in further chapters also are for gaining the internal power.

If you only learn one thing from this chapter, it should be the power punching and striking: this is what will get you out of trouble when attacked by a grappler.

Figure 58

Figure 59

Ultimate Dim-Mak: How to Fight a Grappler and Win

38

Figure 60

Figure 61

Figure 62

CHAPTER
Abstract Antigrappler Training Methods
TWO

It's not good enough to know the techniques to use against a grappler. You must do abstract body training so that the mind and body coordinate in what you are doing. Fortunately, we have simple training methods that will do this for us. Also, it is not good enough to simply have people fight you as a grappler would. This only trains your physical body and not your mind. The theory is that if you train in the dojo using the same techniques that you would on the street, when it comes to the real thing, your body will simply see this as another training session in the dojo and your mind will not activate the reptilian part of the brain. So we have training methods that will allow us to train in "antigrappler" techniques, but will not program our brain to stay in the training mode in the event of a real attack. Sparring, tournament fighting, and so-called full-contact fighting are, in my view, the most damaging impediments to gaining good self-defense methods. Real fighting doesn't happen like it does in those events. We do not have a bell to tell us that an attack is imminent, nor do we have the relative safety of at least *some* rules. In the street, there are *no* rules. Often it is kill or be killed. So when we train in the dojo or in tournaments, our brain knows that it is not for real. We rely upon purely physical attributes, things that we know will work in the ring. Our survival-mode brain, the reptilian brain, is asleep! There is no reason to bring it into the fight because it is not real. Our body remembers these physical moves from our extensive tournament fighting. And when we are really attacked, we do exactly what our mind has been programmed to do. If those techniques do not work, we lose. If, however, we have some abstract way of teaching our brain about real attack situations, we are miles ahead. Some simple training methods prepare our subconscious brain for an attack, and the reptilian part of our brain is then on full alert. The physical movements that we learn from doing these training methods will turn into real self-defense movements, and we will react according to the situation.

We do learn technique, but we should not try to simulate fighting situations by participating in tournaments with rules. The only fighting situations I use are those that really intimidate the student. I wear protective gear and then tell them that if they do not defend themselves, they are going to be knocked out. Then I attack like a wild animal, which awakens the reptilian part of their brains and brings all of their training to life to protect them. I have never lost a student yet using this method of training. The techniques are learned in the dojo in a friendly atmosphere, and learning them becomes a sort of art form. The body likes to do natural, flowing techniques, and so it remembers them more readily. We learn the techniques and then practice them over and over until the mind/body absorbs them and remembers them.

There are training methods from one of my martial arts, taijiquan, which is taught as a technique-oriented fighting method—a sort of prearranged two-person

Abstract Antigrappler Training Methods

set. The student is told that the purpose of this set is to learn about fighting techniques. This is so that the student will not "look" for the antigrappling techniques and try to learn them as such. These methods are built into the pauchui form (cannon fist form, an explosive kata that teaches every possible attack and defense), and they teach us about fighting against a grappler. However, the form must be taught by someone who knows about these hidden training methods. The reason is simple: if the teacher does not know this, he will not be able to correct the student it is done incorrectly, when the student uses the techniques only for what he thinks they are—fighting techniques to be used against different types of attacks. Students like this way of learning the techniques from the taijiquan form. They think they are learning one technique, when all the time they are subconsciously learning another hidden technique that can be drawn upon when a realistic situation arises.

Once the student has learned this form correctly and has practiced for some time, he is told about the hidden reasons for it. By this time the hidden movements will have been learned by the body/mind and will never be unlearned. I will not cover the pauchui form in this book, but I will give some training methods that will have the same effect.

It's also not good enough to simply train in grappling. If you are attacked by a grappler, he is in his element. He has been doing this for many years; you have not. To beat a grappler, we do not train in grappling; we train in our own martial art, the difference being that we now train to use our art against a grappler. You are good at your own martial art. You have put in many hours training, so why change your style just because you want to fight a grappler? Instead, use the many hours of training in your art, but change some things so that it is more effective against a grappler. All good martial arts have this potential. If you cannot fight a grappler using your martial art, then either the martial art is not a good one or your level of expertise in your art is inadequate.

TRAINING METHOD NO. 1: SWINGING

There are two reasons to do training methods. The first is to train the subconscious mind to defend against what a grappler will do to you; the second is to train yourself in what you will do to a grappler.

The "swinging" exercise is from the first category. We must assume the worst scenario, in that the grappler has been able to rush at you and grab you in some way, so we begin the practical training from the bum up. The final stages of training teach you how to prevent the grappler from even touching you, but for now, we must assume the worst.

The grappler, having worked out how you will react to certain attacks through playing mind games, stamping a foot, or moving quickly to see what you will do, , decided upon the old "go high, go low" diversionary tactic and was able to grab you around the waist from behind. He rushed at you high, you overreacted too soon, and he ducked down low and grabbed your waist from behind. This is a normal grappling tactic that works most of the time against people who aren't used to fighting grapplers.

We have the "swinging" method to simulate this. Remember, we aren't learning technique here—your partner has not actually rushed at you—but rather using an abstract training method, a game.

Your partner takes you around the waist from behind and literally hangs off you, placing all of his weight on your waist and pulling down. His hands are locked in the "wrestler's grip" (fig. 63), and his forearms are pressing down on your hip bones (fig. 64).

Even at this relatively easy level, you might find

Abstract Antigrappler Training Methods

43

yourself on the ground, because you aren't used to this kind of pressure from behind. You must not tense up, though—just sink your weight and your energy down, relaxing your upper body totally and relying only on your legs for support. Place your tongue on your upper palate and breathe deeply into your lower abdomen. Pull your chin in and keep your buttocks tucked under, but not tense. Your legs are slightly bent.

This can become a two-way exercise; your partner will find it difficult to hold on for any length of time because he has to hold up his whole weight and his legs are not helping him. Once you have your balance right and are able to stand there calmly, begin to swing your waist from side to side, throwing your partner from side to side as well (fig. 65). Keep your body relaxed and try to feel where your center is; do not allow the weight to pull you backward or forward. Gradually increase the rate and distance of

Figure 63

Figure 64

Ultimate Dim-Mak: How to Fight a Grappler and Win

44

Figure 65

Figure 66

the swinging until your upper body also begins to swing, throwing your arms back on each swing so that your elbows are able to make contact with either side of his head (fig. 66). The actual application of this, of course, is an elbow to the temple (fig. 67). But without the initial "weighting" training, you would be pulled down before you would have time to strike. Do not try to strike with the elbow; keep it abstract. Do not extend the elbow and try to reach his head; just swing your waist, loosen your upper body and arms, and allow your arms to swing naturally to the rear on each side.

Now your partner will up the stakes by trying to pull you backward as well as applying pressure downward. You must relax more, lower your center, and counter this force by swinging your waist violently to either side. This causes him to relax the backward pressure. Remember that your arms have also swung violently in time with your waist, and so your elbow will strike his temple. You will have to "pull" your elbow at this point, as you do not wish to hurt your partner.

To stop you from simply pulling forward when this backward pressure is applied, your partner also pushes forward, trying to push you to the ground. If you are toppled easily, this means that you are simply applying reverse force to his backward attack. You must learn to sink your energy and weight and adjust your center immediately to whatever force is being applied to you. But you not only reverse the force, you must also keep the swinging going, because this is part of your centering process.

To avoid gaining bad habits from the start, if your partner actually gets you on the ground from behind, do not just fall down on top of him, and then get up and begin again. Do something! Never assume that because you are on top of a grappler you have the upper

Figure 67

Figure 68

Ultimate Dim-Mak: How to Fight a Grappler and Win

46

Figure 69

Figure 70

hand. A grappler loves being underneath in the position shown in Figure 68. He'll lock your legs and get the choker or sleeper on you before you hit the ground (fig. 69). So if you think that you are going to fall backward, swing around quickly and violently strike him with whatever weapon you have—preferably to the neck, because this is the most vulnerable point in the animal body. Do not finish there; continue with multiple attacks to the neck until you are sure he is finished. These techniques cannot be used in a tournament, of course, because someone will be killed. We're talking real situations where your life is threatened (figs. 70 through 72). I'll be covering the neck in a later chapter, because it is so important when fighting a grappler or any style of martial artist.

Abstract Antigrappler Training Methods
47

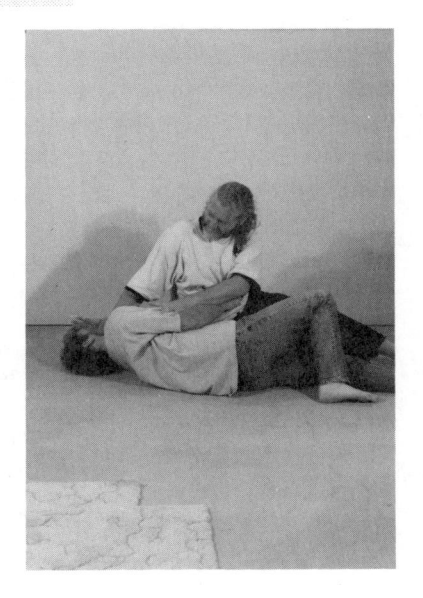

Figure 71

Figure 72

Ultimate Dim-Mak: How to Fight a Grappler and Win

Figure 73

Figure 74

After only a short period of "swinging" training, you'll see how beneficial it will be in fighting against grapplers, not only against grabs from behind but any kind of body pressure. While we're on this subject of grabs from behind, in my training I usually show a couple of methods for getting out of these kinds of attacks. For instance, everyone asks how to get out of a pick-up from behind. Pick-ups are not hard to do, especially if the other person is tense, so the first thing to remember is to relax; do not struggle against being lifted up from behind in preparation for your being thrown down sideways onto the ground. There is not much that the attacker can actually do to you while he is holding you up—he has to do something quickly, because he is getting tired just holding you up (fig. 73). His aim is to throw you down either on your side or on your face so that he can get to you and apply the choker from behind (fig. 74).

Abstract Antigrappler Training Methods

The rule is *grab something!* There is an optimum way to do this, but at the very least, grab his arm tightly (fig. 75). Or grab both of his wrists tightly (fig. 76). Be like a pitbull; do not let go whatever happens. The ideal way of grabbing him is to take your right palm (or left if you wish) and slide it up under his right forearm, while your other hand grabs his right wrist area tightly (fig. 77). You do this the very instant that you feel you are being lifted up, or even as you are grabbed around the waist from behind. Because you have essentially now become a part of the attacker by attaching yourself to him, when he throws you, he will throw himself, leaving you with the advantage (fig. 78).

Figure 75

Figure 76

Ultimate Dim-Mak: How to Fight a Grappler and Win

50

Figure 77

Figure 78

Abstract Antigrappler Training Methods

51

If the grab locks both of your arms as well, all you have to do is open your armpits, rounding out your arms (fig. 79). There is no way your attacker will have better leverage than you in this situation. His hands will not be able to close, and you simply turn your waist violently, as you learned in the "swinging exercise," and strike him with your elbow (fig. 80). Then continue the attack to the neck until he is down. I'll cover some of the major points to strike in a later chapter; however, the point to go for in this instance is Gall Bladder 24 (Gb 24), shown in Figure 81.

Figure 79

Figure 80

52

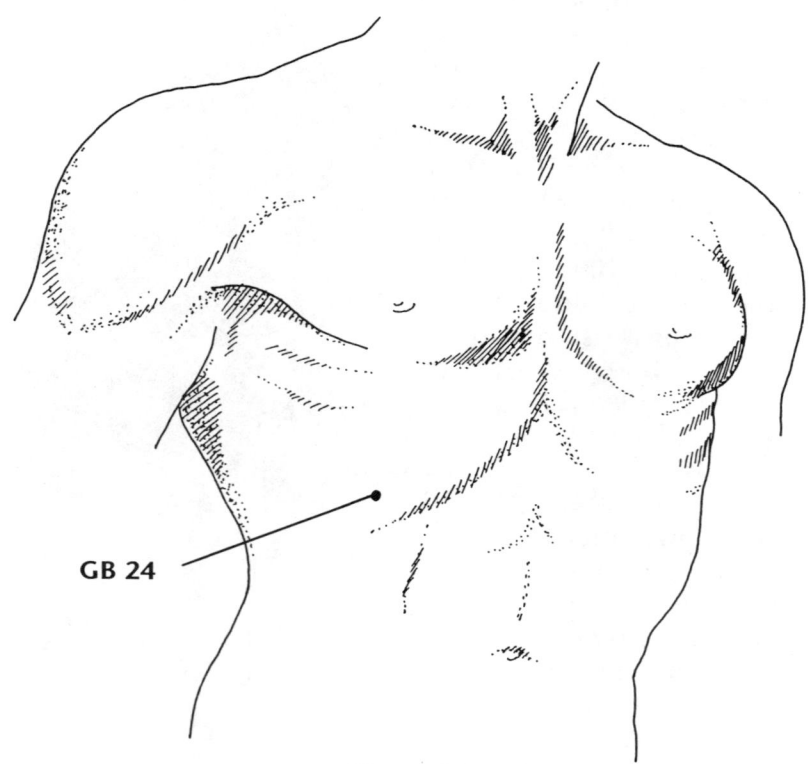

GB 24

Figure 81

From the internal martial art of bagwazhang, we have some simpler ways of getting out of grabs from behind. For a grab from behind where both of your arms are held tightly above the elbows, you might be able to move your palms to a position where you can gouge the quicks of the attacker's fingernails (i.e., the base of the nail, or the cuticle). No one is able to withstand this kind of pain, especially if it is unexpected (fig. 82). This is even easier to do if it is a grab where your arms are outside (fig. 83). Also from bagwazhang comes a more elaborate escape from rear grabs when both arms trapped. You shove your buttocks violently back into your attacker's lower abdomen and thrust both arms up (fig. 84).

Abstract Antigrappler Training Methods

53

Figure 82

Figure 83

Figure 84

Figure 85

Ultimate Dim-Mak: How to Fight a Grappler and Win

LIV 13

Figure 86

Figure 87

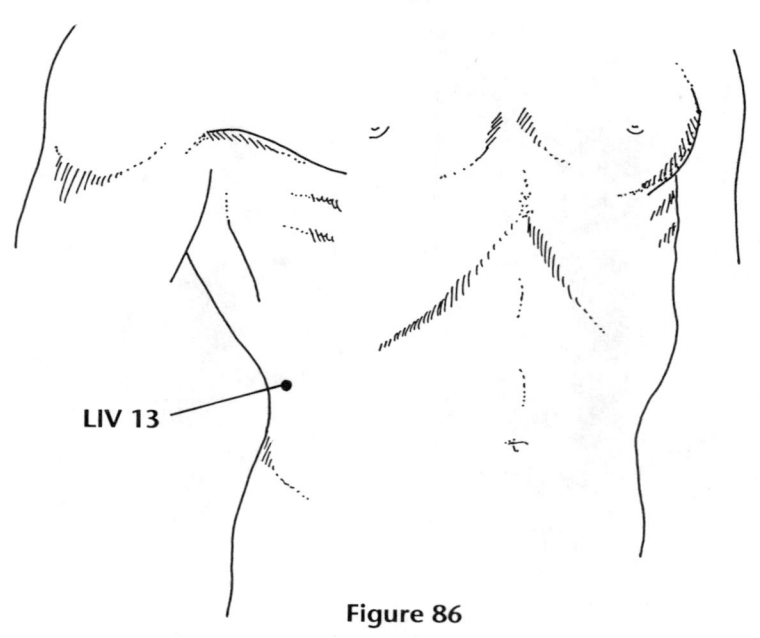

As in Figure 85, turn your waist and strike him in the lower rib area at Liver 13 (Liv 13), the exact location of which is shown in Figure 86. Drop your whole body so that your left foot goes between his legs (fig. 87). Now, as in Figure 88, lift your foot so that you strike him in the groin, or rather at Conceptor Vessel 1 (Cv 1), shown in Figure 89. Lift your body slightly so that you can now attack to the groin again with your palm (fig. 90).

Abstract Antigrappler Training Methods

Figure 88

CV1

Figure 89

Figure 90

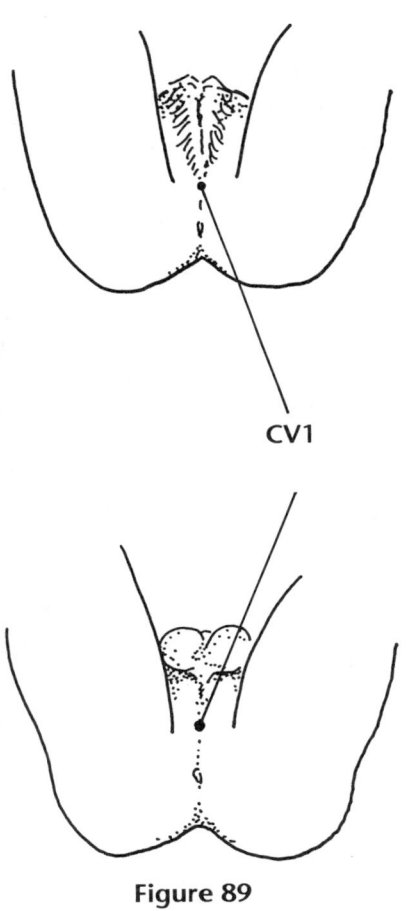

The last couple of techniques require some training, of course, and the less complicated ones are more desirable, but this shows how different martial systems like bagwazhang deal with grapplers. You must be quick, and the more complicated the technique, the slower it becomes. It's no use training in complicated techniques that only work in the dojo; they must also work on the street against real attacks. In the heat of the moment when your adrenal system is working overtime, causing your brain to go haywire, all of those complicated, "beautiful looking" techniques will go right out the window unless you have been training for many years in the system from whence they came under realistic conditions.

**TRAINING METHOD
NO. 2: PUSH HANDS**

I regard locks and holds as the easiest techniques to get out of, but for most people training in the martial arts, this type of attack still presents a problem. This is because most martial arts only train in striking-type attacks—and defending against such attacks. In taijiquan a large part of training is devoted to defense against a grappler, and in particular, arm and hand grabs and locks.

A taiji rule is to go with the flow: allow the attack to dictate what you do in defense; do not force your defense upon the attack no matter what type.

An excellent example of how this rule works is when someone grabs your arm and pulls it, causing you to be thrown past him so that he is able to get an arm lock on you. The best way to get an arm lock of any type is to first draw the person in toward you, moving in toward him as you do. This has the advantages of shortening the distance between you and him, putting him off guard, and facilitating your final method of the lock by jerking his arm. You might be able to grab his arm (fig.

Abstract Antigrappler Training Methods

57

91). You then pull him violently past you (fig. 92). In pulling, you must use your whole body, turning at the waist and using waist power, not just your arm power. As he moves past you, move your own body forward to shorten the gap and, still grabbing with your left palm just above his elbow (pulling points), let go with your right palm, sliding it up under his upper arm to take a reverse figure four lock, leaving your left palm to strike (fig. 93).

Figure 91

The above describes how an arm pull is easily turned into an arm lock. So it is the arm pull that we must defend against to stop the final lock from being activated on us. Remember that you do have another hand. Most martial artists, when their arm is jerked violently, will try to pull their arm back, thus increasing the pressure on their arm and actually helping the attacker!

Most of the pressure is placed on the wrist when it is being pulled. In taiji we have a training method

Figure 92

called "push hands," where we learn to defend against strikes and jerks. The most important thing is to violently rotate the palm that is being pulled or jerked. So if your palm is facing down, which is usually the case (this gives him a better chance of attacking your elbow using a lock), twist your wrist up violently. However, you must do this at the very instant that you feel the wrist grab. It requires some training to gain the awareness and subconscious reaction necessary to do this instantly. When you do this, your arm will be freed immediately, and you will then be able to use the attacker's backward force against him by striking with your other palm (fig. 94).

Taijiquan and bagwazhang have built-in methods, known as "push hands," to enable us to train against arm grabs. There are a number of different types of push hands, ranging from very soft, almost esoteric types to harder, more realistic types.

Figure 93

Figure 94

Abstract Antigrappler Training Methods

It is the more realistic types that I will cover here. Notice that my opening stance is not very low, so as to greatly decrease my chances of being attacked (fig. 95). Many schools of taiji stand in very low, open stances so that their center of balance is lower, giving them more power in attack and defense. But this is not the way it happens in the street, so I tend to use a more natural and normal stance, as if I am just standing there minding my own business when I am attacked (which is more likely to happen).

Figure 95

Using this much shorter almost nonstance makes it much more difficult to defend ourselves, so we get much more realistic training, having to rely upon the waist much more and not just the legs.

I will describe the practice of "single push hands," because it is simpler and is the basis for the more advanced "double push hands." Please note that when someone is just learning taiji in its entirety, the basic push hands using the lower, wider stance is necessary to teach balance and centering. At the more advanced stage, the stance is higher and narrower. For people who need a quick training method, however, I use the more advanced way of single pushing hands.

Many "taijiquan experts" take the movements of pushing hands and use them as defense methods. Push hands was never meant as a literal method of self-defense. It was meant as one of the best methods to gain

60

Figure 96

Figure 97

subconscious or "reflex" self-defense. Hidden within the push hands routine are hundreds of self-defense methods, and because we train in push hands so much, these movements become subconscious without ever having to actually do the self-defense applications. However, I like to show people something of what they are actually learning, so I have included some self-defense applications that represent what you are learning from the push hand movements at a subconscious level. If push hands is taken into the tournament area, then we lose the hidden applications because we are trying to use it to defend ourselves, i.e., the physical movements are used. So we might see someone who is actually attacked in the street trying to defend himself using the p'eng (to ward off) posture (fig. 96). Then he would try to "yield" to this attack by turning his waist to his right (fig. 97), ensuring his defeat. It is okay to use this type of defensive measure in the dojo, where the "attacker" is not really serious. But in the street, his attack would have been upon you before you even had time to go to the next movement.

Push hands should be done with absolutely no competition involved. The two practitioners should not be trying to push each other over. They should exert pressure upon each other, but only to cause the other person's waist to move by itself to defend against the force. We should not have to actually move the force away using our own muscles. The waist should be loose enough and the body centered and grounded enough so that the force of an attack causes us to react automatically and subconsciously, rather than our trying to force the force to do what we want it to do by reacting with a technique that we have thought about consiously prior to the attack. In push hands, we do not learn to yield to an attack; we learn about moving the body so that when a force is put upon it, it will move subconsciously in exactly the right way to deal with this force or attack. Thus, we use the correct defensive measure each time, automatically, without having to think about it first. It also teaches us subconsciously how to reattack using the least possible energy (qi) to gain the greatest possible effect.

You stand opposite your partner, and you both have one foot (we'll use the right one here) slightly forward only slightly of the other. We are not standing in a low, stable stance when attacked, so why use such a stance when we do our push hands? Using a small, more natural stance, we have to rely more upon grounding and balance. This way, when we are attacked for real, we do not have to rely upon big, low stances. The front foot is only about one inch in front of the other, just as if we are standing at a bus stop (fig. 98). (Please note that when teaching beginners who have not even had the most basic of martial arts training, I teach them to use the big, open lowered stance, because their balance is not as yet

Ultimate Dim-Mak: How to Fight a Grappler and Win

62

Figure 98

developed. But as quickly as possible, I take then on to the more advanced higher, shorter stance). The buttocks are tucked under naturally while the weight is lowered slightly (knees are bent slightly). The shoulders are rounded, as is the back. This causes the oncoming force to be grounded through your body. If you, for instance stand with a normal S-shaped back, upright, the force would push straight through you laterally, pushing you backward (fig. 99).

Figure 99

Abstract Antigrappler Training Methods

Figure 100 shows the correct stance for single push hands, wherein we do not use the other hand (although, when we learn the hidden applications, we do make use of the other hand). Nor do we cause the body to lean either left or right, front or back. I have seen many schools of taijiquan whose students "play" at push hands, trying to see who is better at it! There is no reason for this. When the oncoming force is felt, they lean backward greatly, some to the extent of almost doing a back bend! Sure, they defend against the push, but their groin and, in fact, whole body are open to attack. These are the schools that use push hands literally as self-defense measures.

To begin, your partner places his palm onto your right wrist, as in Figure 101. Note that I am weighted on my right foot and my partner is weighted on his left foot. The movement for push hands at this level is not back and forth. We do not make use

Figure 100

Figure 101

of the legs to gain the power; the power comes from the waist. Because of the nonstance, we actually move our body laterally, thus avoiding an attack. So when I move from my right foot to my left foot, I am actually moving from right to left, while my partner is moving from left to right as he "attacks."

My partner now begins to change his weight from his left to right foot, thus giving him more waist power. As he does this, he pushes in an arc from right to left. The apex of this arc goes into my chest (if I allow it to) and then continues on its way out to the other side. I have included several photos to show this arc. We do not attack in a straight line as many schools teach (fig. 102). Rather, we should attack as in the next series of photos, which are included to show you the correct circular line on which to attack. My partner begins his attack by using his waist to turn his palm from his right to left (fig. 103). His hand makes contact on my chest, but

Figure 102

Figure 103

Abstract Antigrappler Training Methods

not straight in; rather, it curves into my chest (fig. 104). I am moved back because of this strike, and his force continues out the other side (fig. 105). If he was to use a straight-in attack and I was not there any more, his forward thrust might force him off balance. When he attacks using lateral waist power, he is not actually leaning forward to gain this attack; his center has only changed from left to right. So if I am not there for his weight to lean upon, he does not fall forward; his energy is centered downward instead. If at any time during this exercise you feel as if you are falling forward, you are doing something wrong. In fact, sometimes if we think that our partner is "leaning" on us, we try to pull our weight out of the way to test his balance.

You feel the force on your right wrist. You hold your position using a strong p'eng-shaped arm, as in Figure 106. Pull your chin in and try to direct the energy through your backbone and to your rear

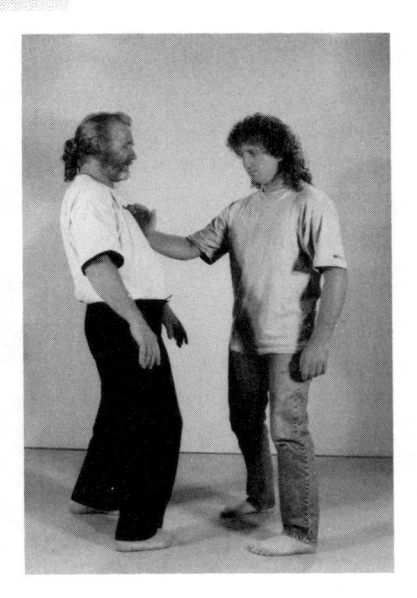

Figure 104

Figure 105

or left foot. (In this case, you also do it with the other foot slightly forward and the other arm forward). Loosen your waist, but do not lose the positioning of your body.

There will be a time of slight tension as his force is directed in to your chest in your center. As you begin to move from the right foot to the left foot, his force will begin to turn your waist to your right. Let it. As your waist turns more, you will gather momentum, and the waist will turn quite quickly to your right as you sit fully onto your left foot (figs. 107 and 108). There should be a feeling of loosening at the end of this action. You have not tried to force his arm, but you have used your body to cause his force to move past you.

It's exactly like pushing on a bicycle wheel that is lateral to the ground. You push to the center and the wheel does not move. Then, when you direct a slight amount of power to one side, the wheel will

Figure 106

Figure 107

Abstract Antigrappler Training Methods

67

begin turning. The wheel does not collapse but just holds its position and turns on its axis, thus defeating the oncoming force. It is the force that causes the wheel to turn, the wheel having no power of its own. We, however, have a head start on the wheel, as we are able to change our weight laterally, thus causing the force to go off to one side enough to begin turning the "wheel."

Do not allow your p'eng arm to collapse. Protect your "garden" with a solid p'eng. This might take some getting used to. Do not bend your wrist; this causes physical weakness and allows your partner to bend your "wheel." Your p'eng hand fingers should point back to your opposite shoulder.

Now it is my turn to push onto my partner's arm. I turn my right palm over so that I am pushing on his right wrist. I do exactly the same thing my partner just did to me, and he reacts in exactly the same way. As I push, he changes his weight to his

Figure 108

Figure 109

left foot, thus causing my power to turn his loose waist to his right (fig. 109).

He returns the push, and we repeat this procedure until we establish a natural rhythm. The main thing for you to learn here is to loosen the waist, but hold the position so that the attack turns your waist and you are not turning it yourself. The main thing for the attacker is to use the power of his waist to do the pushing laterally, as opposed to straight forward. You should feel your waist muscles coming into action, and after a good session of push hands your waist should feel a little sore. What you have done here is to change your weight against a centerline attack, thus causing the attack to miss your center. Your right forearm has warded off the attack, and your body has assumed a position from which you are able to reattack.

Basic push hands is an abstract way of learning about self-defense, allowing the attack to dictate what your body does.

A physical expression of basic push hands translated into a training self-defense method is as follows. You might be attacked with a right straight punch. This can be anything, such as a hand coming toward you. You lean to your left as your right backfist attacks the arm at Colon 10 (Co 10), as in Figure 110. You are weighted on your front foot. This is represented by the initial push on your arm. You change your weight and attack him at Stomach 9 (St 9) with your

Figure 110

left palm (fig. 111). This is represented by your sitting back and turning to your right to avoid the attack.

We now move on. What if your partner should decide to attack your other side, i.e., your left side, instead of attacking directly into your center? This throws a monkey wrench into the works. You have just worked out a nice rhythm, and your partner is going to upset all that. This is important: as you must learn to subconsciously turn to the other side if the attack dictates it. So now your partner directs his attack to your left side. This will be difficult at first, because you are used to turning the other way and sitting back. But now you must "feel" his attack by "listening" with your wrist. His attack will turn your body to your left, and your weight will stay on the front foot (fig. 112). A good way to remember this is to act like you are attacking him with your right shoulder (or left if you are doing it left-handed and left-footed). Now that you have

Figure 111

Figure 112

sapped his energy, his attack has nowhere else to go. You should sit back immediately onto your rear leg, thus taking your body over to your left, and your right palm should slant up to your left as you begin to move, holding a solid p'eng position (fig. 113). Now you simply use your waist to get you turning to your right, and your waist power will help here. Once his hand is past your center, his power will be enough to cause your waist to turn to your right once again (fig. 114). Once the hand is past your center, there should be a kind of release. The waist should fall into place without your having to move it. The movement from center to right should be quicker than from left to center.

Now I am able to push to my partner's left side, and the whole thing is repeated. We have to be aware of not one attack but two different types of attack. But we must not sit there wondering where and when he is going to attack. The body must lis-

Figure 113

Figure 114

Abstract Antigrappler Training Methods

ten all by itself, and the defensive movements must just happen naturally, without conscious thought. Only in this way will you learn to deal with attacks at a subconscious level and not at a conscious, logical level. So if the attacker attacks straight in, you deal with it. If he attacks low and to the side, you deal with it automatically.

A physical expression of the push hands attack to your "other" side is as follows. Remember, do not do these methods while practicing push hands; the "methods" and exercise must be separate training methods. Your partner attacks with perhaps a hook-type of attack, or he may barge at you with both hands open. Your right forearm will *hinge* over to your left, and your left palm will slam down on top of it to attack his forearm (fig. 115). Your weight is forward. Your waist has turned to your left by the action of his attack. You now shake your waist violently to your right, thus thrusting your left fingers into the middle of the side of his neck where it meets the shoulders, at Small Intestine 16 (Si 16), as in Figure 116. Your waist rebounds to your left as your left palm comes back to control his right arm (fig. 117). As your waist again rebounds to your right, your right elbow attacks low to Spleen 17 (Sp 17) at the side of his pectoral (fig. 118). Figure 119 shows the exact location of this point, which is always struck in this direction, from the outside of his body to the

Figure 115

Ultimate Dim-Mak: How to Fight a Grappler and Win

72

middle. Using this method, you do not have to think about the correct direction. This is represented by the defensive move against his push out to your left side in the push hands routine.

Figure 116

Figure 117

Abstract Antigrappler Training Methods

73

Figure 118

SP 17

Figure 119

Begin to sit back onto your left leg. As you do this, your right palm moves under his right arm, taking it over to your right (fig. 120). As you sit back on your left leg, your right palm controls his right arm while your left palm attacks to Si 16. This is represented by your sitting back and taking his arm over to your right in the push hands routine (fig. 121). Now, as your waist turns to your left, your left palm slides down his right arm, controlling it, while your right palm attacks his Conceptor Vessel (Cv 22) point (fig. 122). This is represented by your reattack in the push hands routine.

The third exercise in the push hands routine is a grab and release/attack. You have just turned your waist to your right, taking his attack to your right (fig. 123). You will grab his right wrist just above the wrist and squeeze down on his wrist as your grip increases (fig. 124). You must now shake your waist violently right, left,

Figure 120

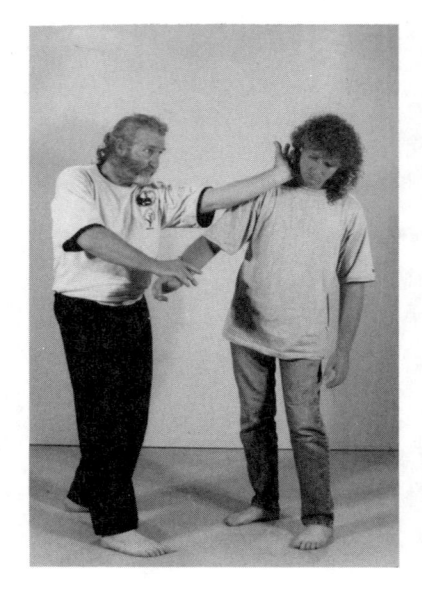

Figure 121

Abstract Antigrappler Training Methods

75

right, which jerks his wrist violently at Heart 5 (H 5) and Lung 8 (Lu 8) points on either side of the inside of his wrist, thus draining his qi dramatically. Your initial grab and jerk must be as explosive as possible so that you are able to grab his wrist. Your partner will try to violently rotate his own palm clockwise at exactly the right time so that your grab will simply slip off (fig. 125).

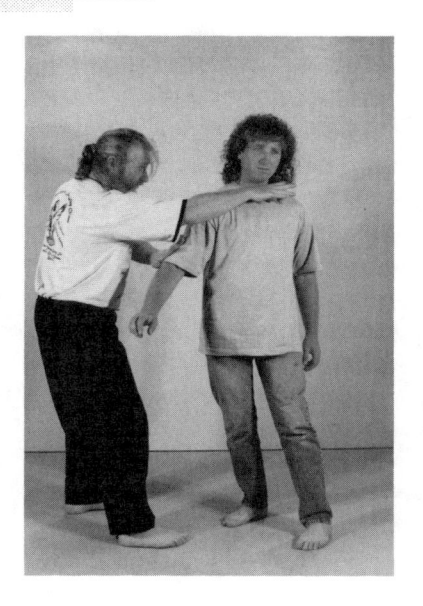

Figure 122

Figure 123

Ultimate Dim-Mak: How to Fight a Grappler and Win

76

Figure 124

Figure 125

Abstract Antigrappler Training Methods

You must not drag your palm back when you rotate it. If you do this rotation correctly, no one will be able to grab your wrist and try to pull you off balance or put a lock on you. You, as the grabber, must actually try to pull the attacker forward, because just holding his wrist will do nothing to him.

When your partner releases your grab, you come back at him with a right palm strike to his face. Remember that he has left his hand there where it was grabbed and has not dragged it back. He will now be able to block your attack upward using his right p'eng hand (fig. 126).

A physical realization of the above push hands method is obvious. He attacks with a right hand. You slam it with your right p'eng hand (fig. 127). You immediately grab his wrist and, using a fa-jing shake of your waist, jerk his wrist violently to your right. This is called *choy qi*, or inch energy (fig. 128). Your left palm now controls his right arm as your

Figure 126

Figure 127

right palm slams into his neck at Cv 22 (fig. 129).

However, if it is you who has been grabbed by the wrist and you have been unable to get out of this hold, taiji does have another training method for those times when your technique is not quite there yet. This is called *da-lu*, or the great repulse.

Da-lu is a rather complicated stepping type of double push hands that utilizes the four corner directions. But we can also use da-lu during single push hands. Da-lu offers a way of saving us when we are caught by a grab and a pull; perhaps the attack was so fast and powerful that it caught us off guard. Rather than just going with the attack and being pulled off balance, we use da-lu. As your partner attacks with a strong pull past himself, do not resist it but allow your body to be pulled in the direction of the pull. Lift your rear foot and place it where the pulling power dictates. In other words, do not force your rear foot down where

Figure 128

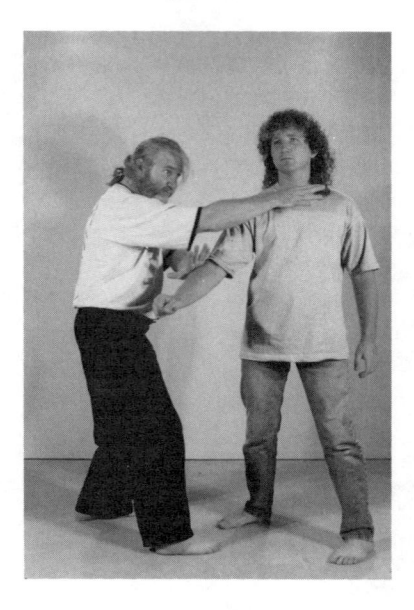

Figure 129

Abstract Antigrappler Training Methods

you want it to go, but allow it to fall when the power has finished.

This gives you the optimum position for reattack. If you were to place your foot before the power had finished, there would still be sufficient power to pull you over sideways, and with both feet on the ground, you would have nowhere to go but sideways (fig. 130).

After your rear foot is placed where it wants to go (fig. 131), push violently with that foot diagonally, forcing your shoulder or elbow into the attacker's chest (fig. 132).

Figure 130

Figure 131

Ultimate Dim-Mak: How to Fight a Grappler and Win

80

Figure 132

TRAINING METHOD NO. 3: ROTATING THE HAND AND STRIKING

From bagwazhang we also have a training method-turned-technique for dealing with arm/wrist grabs. In bagwa we make use of both of the above training methods in that we not only release the wrist but also go with the force, thus putting the attacker even more off guard.

Your partner grabs your right wrist with both of his hands and tries to drag

Figure 133

Abstract Antigrappler Training Methods

you past him (fig. 133). As with the taiji method above, you allow your left foot to be placed where it wants to go for that amount of force and direction (fig. 134).

However, this time you do not only turn the palm to release the grip, you also attack. As your right arm is being pulled, you go with the flow, and at the same time, spear your arm up as it turns toward you. Your palm is facing you as you thrust it up, thus weakening his hold (fig. 135).

Notice that the left palm is drawn back, loaded, ready to strike. The left foot has not yet been placed. As you place your left foot, you lift your right foot. (This is so that you can tell if you are well balanced and have placed your right foot in the correct position.) As your left foot touches the ground, your right knife edge cuts violently down across your partner's right wrist at the small finger side (fig. 136).

Be careful when training with this one: I have twice knocked people out

Figure 134

Figure 135

Ultimate Dim-Mak: How to Fight a Grappler and Win

82

by simply cutting down onto Heart 5. H 5, shown in Figure 137, is an energy drainage point, and striking it can cause great qi loss, resulting in a knockout (KO). The KO is the upper end of the scale; this point usually causes mild energy drainage so that more dangerous points can be set up. Your left palm now comes into play immediately, striking to

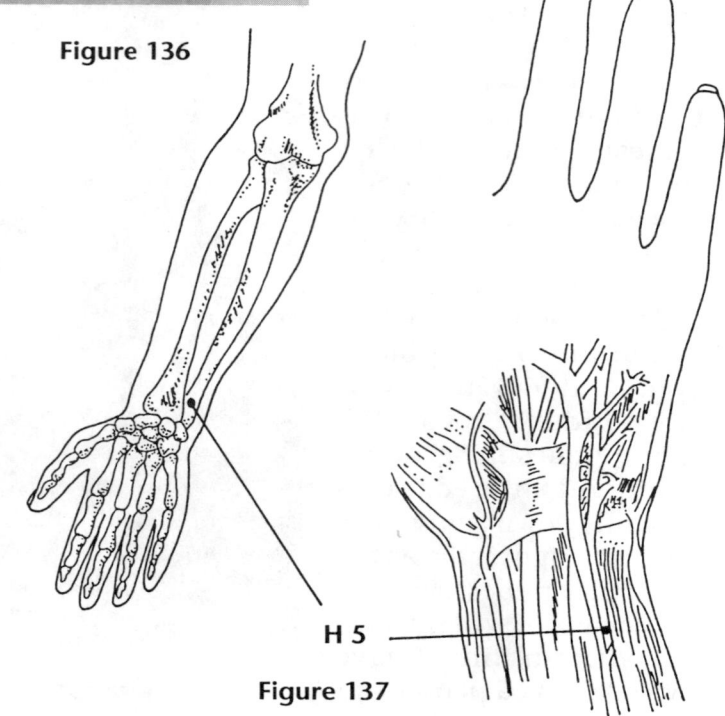

Figure 136

H 5

Figure 137

your partner's temple or Gall Bladder 3 (Gb 3), as in Figure 138.

TRAINING METHOD NO. 4: ADVANCED PUSH HANDS

The above push hands routines will give you the body language/movement and balance to get you out of most grappling-type situations. However, we can now take this exercise a step further. We are still doing what is commonly known as single push hands, but this is a little more advanced.

For the above push hands exercises, the stance was almost directly facing the opponent with one foot only slightly in front of the other. The stance itself does not change, but it looks as if it has. You and your partner should now turn your bodies so that your right shoulder is pointing into your partner's left shoulder and vice versa (fig. 139). You have not taken a wide stance, but rather you have simply turned semiside on to him.

Figure 138

Figure 139

Figure 140

Figure 141

If there is a "fighting stance" in my system, then this would be it. Your waist has to turn a little more to your right (or left if you are doing it on the other side). Your left palm will now come into the play. You now perform the normal pushing, as in the above methods where he pushes on your right wrist, thus turning your waist to your right. Look at the left palm, though: it is held low, in an on-guard position (fig. 140). You continue pushing this way for some time until you are used to the fact that the other hand is also doing something.

Your partner is also able to attack with a low push, to which you answer by taking your right palm low and holding your arm in a hinge position (fig. 141). However, your left palm also moves up to be on guard in front of your face. To move this force out of the way, you turn your waist slightly to your right until his attacking hand simply rolls off to your right. Your partner should not feel any movement,

Abstract Antigrappler Training Methods

because you have moved around the attacking hand but you have not actually moved it (figs. 142 and 143). You now rotate your right palm and reattack, and the pushing continues. You are now able to defend either low or high, depending upon what type of attack it is. But the other hand must move to its opposite position each time. So if your right arm is high, the left is low and vice versa.

We can have many physical manifestations of this type of push hands. Many different "techniques" can be brought in when we actually learn how to use this push hands. However, it is not the actual technique that is important here; it is the body movement and mind coordination that we gain from this exercise.

There are some physical training methods from this type of push hands that we must use to gain an understanding of the basic on-guard stance and its use against a grappler. Your partner attacks high

Figure 142

Figure 143

Ultimate Dim-Mak: How to Fight a Grappler and Win

86

Figure 144

with his right hand. You are in your semiside-on stance as your right forearm slams across to your left and your left palm slams down on top of it (fig. 144). This stops his attack. Immediately, your right backfist slams into his Gall Bladder 1 point (Gb 1), just at the corner of his eye (fig. 145). Remember that it is the shaking of your waist that is causing the fist to be thrust to your right and not just the fact that you throw your right arm out. The power must come from your waist.

Figure 145

Abstract Antigrappler Training Methods

87

From the same type of attack we must also train in a different type of reattack. So after you have blocked his attack using the same method as above, turn your waist slightly to your right to "load" your right hand (fig. 146). Now, with a left-right-left shake of your waist, your right fist rotates and slams into his "mind point" on the side of his jaw, thus preventing the signals from getting from his central nervous system to his brain (fig. 147).

Figure 146

Figure 147

Ultimate Dim-Mak: How to Fight a Grappler and Win

Figure 148

Figure 149

You can also try this method from the "closed side," i.e., he attacks with his left palm. You block in exactly the same way (fig. 148). Now, as you bring your back fist back to his left Gb 1 point, it will have a greater effect because it is striking from the front of his head to the rear, and this produces far more energy loss than just striking Gb 1 straight inward.

From the starting position (fig. 149), your partner again attacks with either a left strike or with both hands toward your head. As in Figure 150, your right palm moves to the outside of his left forearm, striking it just above the elbow at Colon 12 (Co 12). Figure 151 shows the location of this point. See how the body has turned to the right and the weight has shifted to the right foot, thus evading the attack. You again come back with the backfist to his Gb 1 point (fig. 152), with your left palm controlling his left forearm.

Remember that these are all being used as train-

Abstract Antigrappler Training Methods

89

ing methods and are not to be learned as techniques per se. They happen to be very good techniques in and of themselves, but here you are using them as a way to learn about body management. There are many other, much easier techniques that you could have used, but these provide an abstract way of learning about hundreds of techniques without having to actually learn them in a logical way.

Figure 150

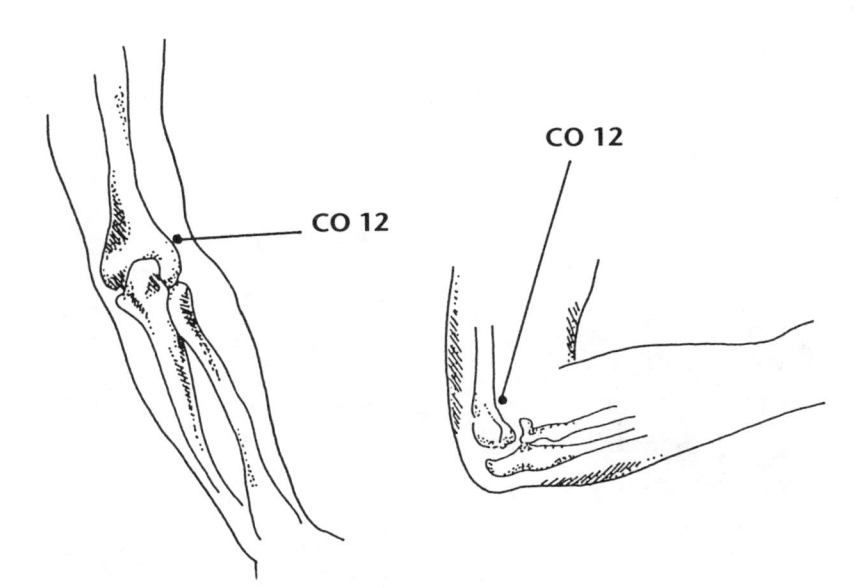

CO 12

CO 12

Figure 151

Ultimate Dim-Mak: How to Fight a Grappler and Win

Figure 152

Figure 153

In all of the above, the back is rounded and the shoulders are spread out to bring forth the "reptilian brain" mode. To put it in Western terms, this stance increases the adrenaline so that, rather than just standing there waiting when attacked, we go out and get the attacker.

For the next method, your partner either strikes with a right or comes at you with both hands. You will block his attack using the two-handed method (fig. 153). You then shake

Abstract Antigrappler Training Methods

your waist violently left and right, grabbing his right wrist at the energy drainage points of Heart 5 and Lung 8 (Lu 8), which are

Figure 154

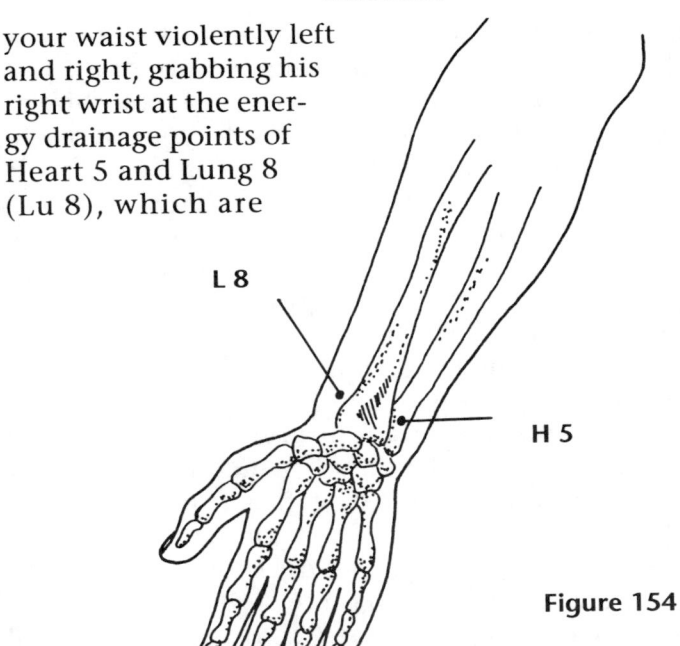

illustrated in Figure 154, and striking him with your right palm just on top of his hip bone into the girdle meridian. Remember that the grab of his right wrist is also a strike—a negative strike that drains energy. So, as Figure 155 shows, the grab must also be connected to the shaking of the waist.

From the simple methods of fighting given above, you will be able to

Figure 155

work out for yourself many other applications of the p'eng/hinge method. These training methods give you the foundation upon which to build your repertoire of subconscious reactions. You must change your stance to the left foot forward and perform all of these methods that way as well. At an advanced stage, your partner will be attacking you from all angles and with different types of attacks. You must also move in. This is the most important part of your training. Do not just stand there waiting for your partner's power to be at its fullest when he attacks. He waits, outside of your attack range, and then he moves in slowly, ready to attack. As soon as he is within your range, you must attack him, even before he has a chance! But if he does attack, the principle is the same. Attack him the very instant he gets within your attack range, so you will be moving before he gets close enough to hit you. Your attack range does not change. This means that if you can touch his arm (or leg if it is a kick) about halfway down his forearm, you can attack him. He will probably be moving in, so the short distance from middle forearm to his centerline will be almost nonexistent. And if you used one of the arm-slamming methods, this will also put his timing and power right off. Before he knows it, your palm is striking one of the dangerous points in his neck. So it's important to work out your own "attack range" subconsciously. To do this, you simply watch people. Out in the street, on a bus or train, you see with your peripheral vision. As you detect someone coming within your attack range, you recognize this as the time to attack. Soon, you will be doing this automatically.

There is one more method of using p'eng/hinge push hands, and it involves your attack range. Have your partner walk around in an on-guard stance, from a great distance to within your attack range. The very instant that he comes within your attack range, your right (or left if in a left stance) fist strikes his face or neck using the snapping twisting punch. You can do this to his

Abstract Antigrappler Training Methods

93

open side, as in Figure 156, or you can do a simultaneous arm strike and neck strike by doing it to his "closed" side (fig. 157).

Figure 156

Figure 157

TRAINING METHOD NO. 5: AWARENESS TRAINING USING ONE MITT

Later in this book you will see that awareness is one of the major weapons when fighting against a grappler. Relaxation is a big part of becoming aware of what is happening around you. Awareness does not simply mean knowing that certain things are happening. It means that you also react subconsciously and instantly. The grappler's toolbox is loaded with tools that play upon a fighter's unawareness. He is able to rush at us and have us in a lock before we have time to react. This is where the grappler is superior. He is not afraid of your kicks and punches because he probably has never come up against someone who is able to actually kick or punch, so he will wait for his moment and then rush at you while you are thinking about what to do.

All of the internal martial arts require heavy training in gaining this necessary awareness to strike the moment the attacker moves even one inch. There are certain training methods from the internal martial arts that anyone can use.

The first awareness exercise trains the peripheral vision. This is absolutely necessary because if you are seeing with your "focus" vision, you will focus too late and your attacker will be upon you. Your partner holds one hard striking mitt, while you stand in front of him within striking distance. You close your eyes, and your partner moves the mitt to a different position so that you do not know where it will be when you open your eyes. For instance, he might move it to your left side near your face. You open your eyes but do not turn your head to look at the mitt. Using your peripheral vision, you will see the mitt just to your left. You now turn your waist and strike the mitt with as much power as you can (fig. 158). Your head turns as you strike the mitt, but not before. This teaches you to strike when you see it rather than turning to focus first and then striking.

This exercise also teaches you to use the right tool for the job, the one that will give you the most power over the shortest distance. In the above case, you would not, for instance, strike using your left fist, as this would require you to draw your left fist back and then turn your waist back to your right before striking. Using your right fist, you can simply turn your waist to your left instantly and strike without losing power.

You should train this way until you can decrease the time between when you open your eyes and when you strike as much as possible without losing power. It's no good to be able to hit the mitt with blinding speed if you are not going to do any damage. Have your partner hold the mitt within range of your hands at first (up and down, etc.). Then, as you become more competent at using your peripheral vision, have him hold it either closer or farther

Figure 158

Figure 159

Figure 160

Figure 161

away, forcing you to strike with your elbow or your foot, for instance. When the mitt is low and closer to your feet, use, in particular, an upward toe strike, as in Figure 159. This will help in combating a grappler when he comes in low to tackle you. Also have your partner hold the mitt facing up, close to either side of your body so that you can use a downward elbow strike (fig. 160) or a slamming palm. (fig. 161).

Now you must increase the number of strikes. Not only will you strike the mitt with your fist, but you will follow up with an elbow strike and a knee strike. Try all sorts of combinations, but be sure not to lose power. Only use strikes that flow naturally on from the last strike. For instance, you would not use a knee strike right after a fist. You would first use an elbow and then drag the mitt down onto your knee.

The next phase is to have your partner hold the mitt too far away for you to reach without moving in. Remember, your partner has not actually attacked you with the mitt; he is just standing there. So to establish good habits right from the start, do not attack the mitt if it is too far away to touch without moving forward. Practicing this increases your awareness of when to strike. So in this exercise you do not know where the mitt will be, you do not know whether you should strike at it or not, and you do not know which weapon to use—feet, hands, elbows, knee, and so on.

The next area is probably the hardest, but it will bring you the greatest rewards if you practice a lot. Your partner says "go," which is the signal for you to open your eyes. At that point, he will either move in on you from a distance or stay out of your range. You must decide instantly whether to move forward, which is what you must do if he is moving forward, or to stay still, which is what you must do if he does not come within range of your strike.

**TRAINING METHOD NO. 6:
FINGER POKING EXERCISE**

This exercise is quite simple, but you gain much in the way of awareness and the use of peripheral vision from it. Stand in front of your partner and close your eyes; your partner moves his body so that his head is within your reach, but perhaps at a different angle (he might stand to your side slightly). Open your eyes upon his command and immediately, without turning your head or focusing on his nose, poke your index finger onto the tip of his nose (fig. 162). Your mind is seeing his whole body, while your eyes are looking, but not focusing, 45 degrees to his body. Try this exercise. Look at something in the distance. Focus your eyes on something so that your brain also sees it. Now, without turning, make your brain look at your partner without turning your head or eyes, and then go back to the distant object. This teaches you to see with your brain. You must also have *intent* when you poke your finger. If you feel that you will not be able to do this and perhaps do it timidly as a result, you will not strike the tip of his nose. But with intent, you will be able to do this every time. Breathe out and push out your lower abdomen as you do this (reverse breath), to give you the intent that leads into the reptile brain mode. Do not strike your finger crosswise until it just strikes his nose; your finger must poke outward so that the tip makes contact with the tip of his nose. Do this softly; you do not want to poke him in the eye or, worse still, up his nose! You will be surprised at how accurate you will become in a short time. Remember, do not turn your head or look out of the corner of your eyes.

Figure 162

TRAINING METHOD NO. 7: USING TWO MITTS

This training method uses two hard punching mitts. Your partner holds each hand so that you are able to reach them when you strike. (This method also lends some training to your partner in that he will have to be quite aware of which mitt is being struck first. But before we get on to that area we will work at a basic level.) Strike his right mitt, as in Figure 163. The instant that you strike the

Abstract Antigrappler Training Methods

mitt, your partner moves the other mitt, which you have to strike instantly wherever it is (fig. 164). You must not look for the second mitt, but do exactly the same with your eyes as when you were using only one mitt. Do not look first and then strike; see the mitt with your peripheral vision and immediately strike it as you turn your head.

When you become more at ease with this exercise, your partner will be able to move the mitt that is not being struck without waiting. So you will be striking each mitt just after it has moved. One mitt moves, and you strike it with whatever weapon is the most appropriate in terms of providing the most power and speed. Then the other mitt will have moved, so you strike it, and so on. Your partner's training comes in when you are striking the mitts so quickly that his awareness has to be in top gear to keep up with you. He will find himself moving the wrong mitt at the wrong time, and so on.

Figure 163

Figure 164

TRAINING METHOD NO. 8: VOICE MEDIATOR

The voice is a semiabstract thing that we can use to increase our awareness and lessen the gap between thought and action. Obviously, it would be advantageous to be able to move at the very instant that the mind thinks about it. However, there is a huge gap between the two, and this can mean the difference between being beaten or winning a confrontation.

What happens when you are startled? You make a sound, a scream maybe, and then you react to whatever it was that startled you. The voice moves first. If we can get the voice to move with the body, then we have increased our awareness. The voice is a kind of mediator between abstract (thought) and physical (movement), so we begin with the voice.

Your partner stands opposite you at arm's length. You will be using your peripheral vision to see his every move, even if it is only a blink of an eye. In the beginning your partner makes his movements quite gross, like raising his arm to strike you. The instant that you notice his movement, you should make some kind of sound, such as "huh." With practice, you will be "huhing" at the same time that your partner begins to move. Notice his head—that triangle that is formed from each shoulder to the crown (fig. 165). There is no way that anyone can attack you in any way without that triangle

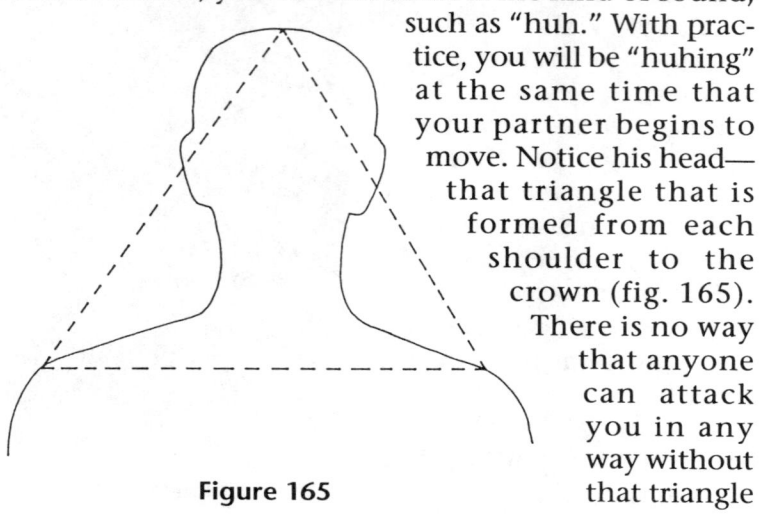

Figure 165

Abstract Antigrappler Training Methods
101

moving. The shoulder will move if it is a hand attack, and the head will move if it is a foot attack.

Your partner begins with large movements until he can no longer fool you. Then his movements become smaller and quicker so that you are making the sound to his every move.

The next step is for you to try to touch his moving part as it comes toward you and at the same time that your voice makes the sound. In other words, your hand and voice are reacting at the same time

Figure 166

(fig. 166). You can try this on a bus or train while commuting to work. The instant someone else in the bus moves, perhaps to scratch his or her head, make your inaudible sound. (I say inaudible because you don't want to be thrown off the bus for making strange sounds when people move!) Try to take in everyone in the bus using your peripheral vision.

In no time at all, you will be reacting to movement using your peripheral vision subconsciously. You'll be walking down the street, for instance, and you'll be moving your body subconsciously long before someone comes near you, or you will be avoiding that swinging arm as someone else rushes past you.

• • •

All the above training methods are to get you to move at the very second that an attack is launched.

You do not wait for the fist to be in your face, but rather you move at precisely the same moment that your attacker does. This is the only way to defeat a grappler—to do something that he does not expect. The grappler rushes at you, expecting you to be there, but you are not. You are in his face with a devastating attack of your own.

TRAINING METHOD NO. 9:
DEAD-ARM TRAINING METHODS

First, using your left hinge forearm, you should block/slam your partner's right attack (fig. 167). Your arm should be totally dead. You are only using the waist to gain the power, and not the muscles in your arm. Now, lean your elbow on top of his. Your partner will have to hold his arm fairly firmly (fig. 168). Your partner holds his left hand so that you are able to strike it. Be careful doing this, and let your partner know that a fairly strong force is about to strike his palm. Using your waist power, shake your waist to your left, causing your left palm to be slammed violently into his left palm (fig. 169). The shaking of your waist continues to your right, and your left palm just flops down onto his forearm (fig. 170). You must not use muscle power to lift your left palm, but rather use only the waist to cause centrifugal force.

Figure 167

Abstract Antigrappler Training Methods

103

Figure 168

Figure 169

Ultimate Dim-Mak: How to Fight a Grappler and Win

Figure 170

Figure 171

This first exercise will teach you to use relaxed strikes rather than tense ones, thus giving much more power for strikes such as the neurological shutdown strike that follows.

Your partner attacks with perhaps a right straight. Use your waist power and a little controlling of your left palm to slap his inside forearm (fig. 171). Using the power of your waist only, shake your waist, causing your left backhand to be slapped into the side of his face exactly as shown in Figure 172. This will cause a KO by neurological shutdown. This training method teaches us to use subconscious loose strikes to anywhere at any time, thus giving great power and qi transference.

TRAINING METHOD NO. 10: BUMPING

This training method is one of the most beneficial to martial artists in general, as well as those wishing to learn how to fight a grappler. It offers a number of benefits, such as building up the correct parts of the body for fighting grapplers, working the correct muscle groups to develop powerful strikes, and giving the necessary body contact for gaining a more realistic view and feel of fighting.

Stand with one foot forward while holding a p'eng arm (fig. 173). You must have that same feeling in your arm that you do for the push hands: not rigid, but not totally relaxed. You must use only the triceps

Figure 172

Figure 173

when contact is made. Your palm must be relaxed, as well as your forearm.

Your partner runs at you from a distance, with both arms stretched out. His arms are stretched tightly. He runs into your p'eng arm and makes contact onto your wrist and forearm with both hands, as in Figure 174. Using your subconscious brain, move forward to meet him at the right time of contact to try to bounce him away (fig. 175). Do not allow your arm to collapse upon impact. Do this 10 times and then change arms and feet and perform the exercise 10 times again.

The next bumping exercise is called "the goats butting." As in Figure 176, place your arms and hands so that your right wrist is touching the back of your partner's right wrist, your left palm is touching his right elbow, and his left palm is touching your right elbow. Now each of you sits back onto your back legs and draws your arms

Figure 174

Figure 175

Abstract Antigrappler Training Methods

back to your left (fig. 177). This represents the two goats getting ready to butt. Next you both bring your weight forward and turn your waists to the front, making contact at those same places and trying to knock each other backward (fig. 178). After you have had enough of this side, change feet and arms so that you can do it on the reverse side.

TRAINING METHOD NO. 11: DIM MAK GRAPPLING

Figure 176

I have called this next training method "dim-mak grappling" because it uses dim-mak fighting methods in the first instance to allow you to then use some grappling methods yourself. They should be used as training methods first, hence my including them in this chapter. However, as with all training methods, they can be used as fighting methods as well.

Grappling techniques will not work against a grappler. He is used to

Figure 177

being grappled, and your own knowledge and experience will probably not be good enough to straight-out grapple with him. So if you must use a grappling technique, lock, or hold, you must either stun him or knock him out first. When he awakes, you will have the lock on tightly, and his energy will have been drained sufficiently for you to hold him.

This next training method embodies many different methods of dealing with grapplers. Within this method there are many "nontechniques" that can be used separately.

You are attacked with something to your head, such as a grappler's two-handed attack, or a single strike. You get inside of his attack so that you can use the double p'eng method to attack to his St 9 point (fig. 179).

There are several things you can do now.

Figure 178

Figure 179

Abstract Antigrappler Training Methods
109

1) Take his elbow with your right palm and his wrist with your left, as in Figure 180. Pull/jerk your right palm and push your left palm to end up turning his body so that you are now facing the back of him (fig. 181). Slide your right forearm under his right forearm and up onto his neck (fig. 182). You now have a reverse hammer lock, which will break his arm if necessary. Now take your left palm and place it around his neck until you can grab it with your right palm (fig. 183). You now have a sleeper hold.

Figure 180

Figure 181

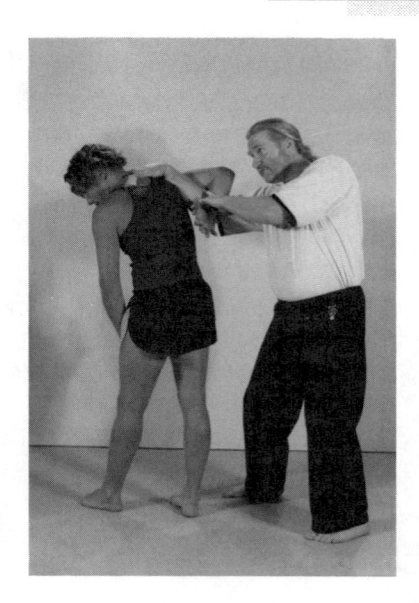

Figure 182

Figure 183

Abstract Antigrappler Training Methods
111

2) Grab his right wrist with your left hand and place the back of your right wrist into the crease of his elbow (fig. 184). As you do this, still facing the opposite direction, place your right leg (toes only touching the ground) between his legs, with the back of your right knee touching the back of his right knee. (fig. 185). Now, twist your waist violently to your rear, bending his wrist back with your left hand while pushing forward with your right forearm into the crease of his elbow. Straighten your right leg violently, which causes his right leg to be struck violently, throwing him off balance. Your right forearm strikes/pushes into the crease of his elbow (a "come with me" point), and your left palm bends his arms so that the attack is not a pull from the wrist but rather from the elbow (fig. 186).

Done correctly, this

Figure 184

Figure 185

Ultimate Dim-Mak: How to Fight a Grappler and Win

112

Figure 186

Figure 187

should lift him off the ground almost laterally so that he ends up at your feet. You have twisted 180 degrees to the rear, but it doesn't finish here. If there is only one person fighting you, you should follow him to the ground. If there is more than one person, you should finish him off with the throw and get on with the others. Since there is only an attacker in this case, follow him to the ground. Your right knee slams down onto his "girdle meridian," which runs around his waist and hips. You should strike with your knee just above his right hip bone. Your right fingers will poke into and down into his eye sockets at the Stomach 1 (St 1) points (just inside his lower eye bone). Your left palm still controls his qi drainage points, H 5 and Lu 8, and your left big toe presses hard up into Heart 1 in his armpit (fig. 187).

Abstract Antigrappler Training Methods

The takedown has happened in one clean sweep. The spin around that you did naturally moves into the takedown, and all of the other attacks will naturally follow.

3) As soon as you have pulled him around by pulling his right elbow and pushing with your left palm, you can jerk him into your chest and put both arms around his neck in a choker hold (fig. 188). The method of this should be as violent as possible to stop any counter should your St 9 shot not work or only stun him. Should he still try to do something, like striking you in the groin, you should shake his head violently to stop this attack.

Figure 188

4) From this initial double p'eng attack, you should place your left palm under his right arm and onto his neck (fig. 189). Place your right palm on top of

Figure 189

Ultimate Dim-Mak: How to Fight a Grappler and Win

114

your left and, using that leverage, bend him down so far that his head strikes the ground, as in Figure 190. ("You now have a long arm bar hold.")

5) Pull him around again and slide your left palm up under his right forearm so that it ends up on his right shoulder. You now have great leverage on his shoulder tendons and muscles and can control him easily, leaving your right palm free to strike again (fig. 191). You now have a hammer lock or reverse figure four lock.

Figure 190

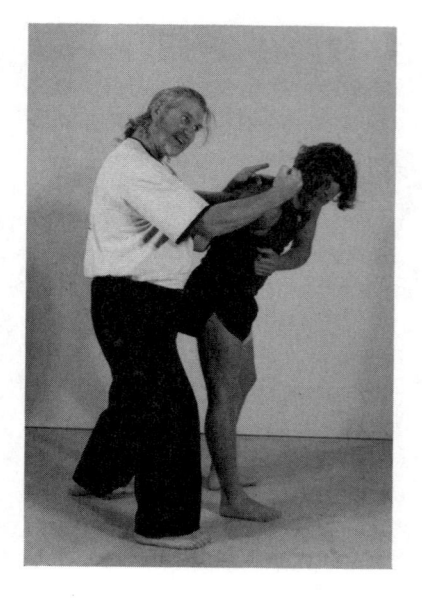

Figure 191

Abstract Antigrappler Training Methods

These five methods could also have been initiated by using the method known as "dragon prawn boxing." Your partner attacks with a right, and you slap the inside of his right wrist at Neigwan with your right palm (fig. 192). Your left palm immediately comes up underneath your right palm to take over the block, as in Figure 193. Your right palm is now free to attack to St 9 or anywhere on the neck (fig. 194). From here you can execute any of the above methods.

Figure 192

Figure 193

The above training methods will give you all that is necessary to take care of any grappling type of attack, and also any type of "normal" attack. However, you must train in these methods to enable not only your body but, more importantly, your mind to change habits. Remember the old Chinese saying: "Allow him to come to you, but you get there first."

Figure 194

CHAPTER

Fa-Jing Ch'uan Training Methods

THREE

Although each of the following 10 fa-jing ch'uan (explosive energy fist) methods is used as fighting methods by itself, the way we learn about them is one of the best known training methods for about "no form" or "no mind." This is where we learn to defend ourselves by adjusting automatically to what the opponent is attacking us with; so we do not use such and such a technique regardless of what is being thrust upon us, but rather we react to an attack with the correct defensive measure.

Bruce Lee's way was called "the way of the intercepting fist," or jeet kune do. This means that when the attack is on its way, we must intercept it before it gets to us. This could mean that we kick his knee as our attacker comes forward, or we simply attack his face as he attacks with a punch. All of the internal arts are alike in this aspect: we are taught never to move back, but to move in, intercept, and attack to the center. This is basic to all of the internal arts. But it is my belief that what we learn first, especially in our childhood, is what influences us most throughout our lives. Bruce Lee was taught t'ai chi ch'uan by his father, and what

Bruce taught incorporated many of the t'ai chi principles. It does not matter what physical arts he taught, the basis was his t'ai chi.

The following methods are the most effective for learning about this subconscious fa-jing way of defense against a grappler in particular, but they work for any type of attack.

To do these methods, you must have internal energy or strength and the ability to do fa-jing attacks. So, in learning these methods, we also learn about the most important aspects of fighting against a grappler, that of explosive energy.

Fa-jing ch'uan is the name I use for my own fighting art. Meaning explosive energy boxing (literally fist), it has its roots in t'ai chi ch'uan and bagwazhang, two of the internal classical fighting arts of China. The following methods/movements are those I teach to beginning students. This type of training provides an instant way of learning fa-jing without much need for talking. It provides physical exercise and stamina. It gives the student extreme power and speed and the ability to attack when being attacked and strike at the most vital of dim-mak points.

Fa-jing ch'uan is also the foundation for learning dim-mak only (i.e., when someone wishes to learn about dim-mak without learning the original dim-mak forms from t'ai chi ch'uan). Perhaps I am teaching a group of karate people who do not wish at that time to totally embrace t'ai chi ch'uan, because it is time consuming. Usually people find that it is essential to learn the whole system from scratch in order to learn dim-mak properly. But the fa-jing ch'uan provides a great understanding even without learning t'ai chi from scratch. (I am currently producing a new videotape series called *Fa-Jing Ch'uan: Dim-Mak from A to Z*. The fa-jing ch'uan exercises are the first things I show on these tapes.)

FA-JING CH'UAN TRAINING METHOD NO. 1

You stand in a normal p'eng-hinge stance, or ready position, with your right foot forward. P'eng-hinge is not really a stance, as such. The feet are only shoulder width apart, one foot in front of the other, just as if you are standing at bus stop. Your right arm is slanting slightly upward, relaxed, while your left arm is hanging down, p'eng and hinge respectively (fig. 195). This is the ideal way to stand to be protected from any type of attack. This stance can be lessened so that it does not look like an on-guard stance (fig. 196). Here, the right palm is the p'eng and the left the hinge. At any time both arms can move outward instantly (fig. 197).

Your body must be relaxed, like a rag doll. If you turn your waist suddenly, the upper body resembles a rag doll shaking to and fro. Without this looseness, you will

Figure 195

Figure 196

Figure 197

Figure 198

not be able to perform fa-jing ch'uan. I'll give the moves slowly so that you can see the minute movements of waist, feet, and upper body. However, each move is done at an extremely explosive speed and takes only a split second to execute. If the arms are at all stiff, you will not get it. If you are feeling tired and lack energy, this is also not a good exercise to do; you must do some qigong (Chinese breathing exercises) or some t'ai chi forms in order to get your energy levels up. When you begin with a good amount of qi, you will begin to add to this energy by performing "fa-jing ch'uan," but there must be something there to begin with. Otherwise it's a bit like trying to start a car with a weak battery: it only depletes the battery more. If the battery has at least some energy, the car will start and then begin to charge the battery itself.

Shake the waist left, right, left, right, and then take one step forward with the right foot and slide the

Fa-Jing Ch'uan Training Methods

left foot forward one step as well. Turn your waist slightly to your left, which will take your palms to your left (fig. 198). As you step forward with your right foot, turn your waist to your right, thus taking both palms to your right (fig. 199). Place your right foot and, as the weight rolls onto it, the waist snaps left, the right fist snaps into a punch and the waist snaps to the right (fig. 200). Notice that the right fist begins with the palm facing slightly down and, as it attacks, is snapped over, ending up palm slightly upward. There is such a snapping action on the punch that you actually hear the fist *snap* into position. The fist forms only upon impact and is the "tiger paw" type (fig. 201). It is very difficult to take photos of the movements done at full speed, but in Figures 202 through 204 have tried to show this.

Repeat this exercise to the end of your training space. When you get to the end with your right foot forward, your left

Figure 199

Figure 200

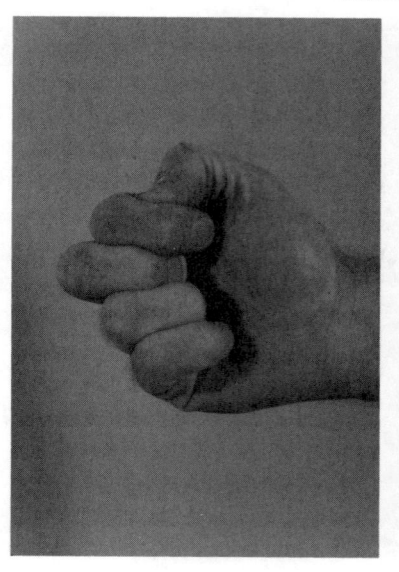

Figure 201

Figure 202

Figure 203

Figure 204

Fa-Jing Ch'uan Training Methods

palm pokes underneath your right wrist (fig. 205). Swivel on your heels, allowing your left palm to lead so that you end up facing the opposite direction, ready to do the whole thing on the reverse side (fig. 206).

Figure 205

Figure 206

Figure 207

Figure 208

Working with a Partner

Each of the fa-jing ch'uan exercises must also be practiced with a partner. Once you think that you have mastered the solo exercise, your partner simply stands in front of you in a sort of on-guard stance, as if he is going to rush at you as a grappler would (fig. 207). It does not have to be a grappler's stance; it can be any on-guard stance, represented by a punch, etc.

Now you will use what you have just learned in a practical way. You learn to "open up" an attacker so that you can get at his vital points, particularly in the neck. On your first shake to your left, you slam the outside striking bone of your left palm (fig. 208) into his right wrist at Neigwan, or Pericardium 6 (Pc 6), located one hand's width back from his wrist band on the inside of his forearm. This is the set-up point that causes the main strike to be much more dangerous and effective (fig. 209). You must strike with fa-jing power so that his arm is jolted outward. If his arm is still in contact with your left palm, then you have not used fa-jing power.

Immediately following the setup, your waist turns to your right, causing your right outside palm striking point to attack to his left Neigwan point. As you do this, your right foot steps to close the gap (fig. 210). Your left foot touches the ground, and as your weight comes forward, your right tiger paw fist attacks to his Conceptor Vessel 22 (Cv 22) point in the pit of his neck (fig. 211). This whole method has taken only a split second to execute and should be done with a "pah" sound (not three pah sounds, but only one sound for all three movements; that's how fast it is).

Practice the first two defensive strikes first, getting them down to a split second. But remember, you must not simply open each arm to the left and right respectively; this is not fa-jing. Each palm must remain in its beginning position, with the body's turning causing

Figure 209

Figure 210

each palm in turn to strike the inner arm. True fa-jing comes from the waist turning violently to each side and then returning to center. The final attack to Cv 22 should also be caused by the waist and not just the arm. Cv 22 is an extreme death point. When struck, it causes death, with revival methods being useless.

The two-person exercise must also be practiced up and down the training hall on both sides, so your partner must move backward after each attack. You must not actually have your partner attack you. There is the danger here of just standing there waiting for him to come to you. This is incorrect body technique. When attacked, we move in toward the opponent and not back, or we just stand there waiting for his full power to reach us. So, in moving in to your partner, you get into good habits right from the beginning. You are attacking him the instant he raises his hands to attack.

Figure 211

FA-JING CH'UAN TRAINING METHOD NO. 2

This next exercise teaches probably the most important and deadly point of Stomach 9 (St 9). This is the easiest of points to get at, especially in a grappling situation. Note how easy it is to strike to this point when someone attacks with either a hook punch or a rush in, à la grappling (fig. 212). As he rushes in, I simply lift both arms, and the left one strikes to the inside of his right

Fa-Jing Ch'uan Training Methods

forearm while the other fits perfectly into St 9 at the side of the neck. All I did was lift my arms, and he ran into them. The direction is correct, the power is right (he dictated this by running in), and I did not have to do anything but lift my arms.

St 9 (fig. 213) has an immediate effect in that it causes a knockout or death if struck hard enough. I have covered this point in great detail in my earlier books and videos, but in a nutshell, just under St 9 lies the carotid sinus, a "baroreceptor" that dictates how your heart controls high blood pressure. In a normal situation, where someone's blood pressure rises simply as a result of eating the wrong food or stress, the carotid sinus registers high blood pressure, sending a signal to the cardioinhibitory center in the brain, which in turn sends a signal to the heart via the vagus nerve, telling it to either slow down or, in the case of extremely high pressure, to stop. In an abnormal situation where someone has been struck at St 9, the carotid sinus registers extremely high blood pressure,

Figure 212

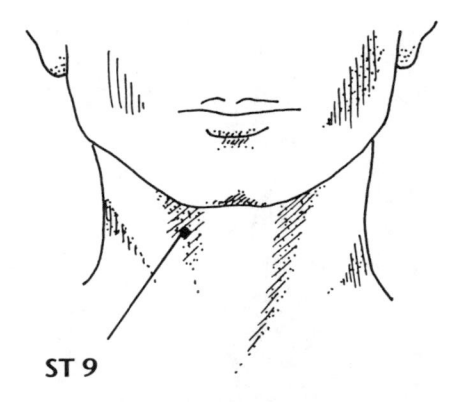

ST 9

Figure 213

telling the heart to stop in order to lower the pressure. But as the person does not actually have high blood pressure, he goes into knockout. The heart will eventually restart unless the point is struck too hard, in which case it will not.

St 9 will work regardless of any set-up points that are struck prior to striking it. However, if we use a set-up point strike, it works even better. So rather than just blocking the attacker's arms as he rushes in, we strike to points on the arms that will work as set-up points for St 9. The more set-up points we can strike before getting to St 9, the better.

Again, the waist is the controller, turning left, right, left, and then back to the right to center. It happens in an instant. The waist turns to your left as your right palm opens and is also moved to your left by the action of your waist (fig. 214). As your waist turns to the right, your left palm comes up underneath your right wrist to also strike out to your left (fig. 215). Both wrists have flexed either positive (the right palm flexes back) or negative (the left palm flexes down, or is limp). As you take a step forward with your right foot, your waist turns to your right, causing your right palm to strike out to your right with a positive or yang-shaped palm (fig. 216). You place your right foot, and as your weight comes forward onto it, your right palm turns over to face upward and strikes forward with the *shuto*, or

Figure 214

Fa-Jing Ch'uan Training Methods

knife edge (fig. 217). Your waist has turned to your left and then to the right to center again. You must do this exercise on the other side once you have reached the end of your training space, as in the first exercise.

All of this has taken a split second to execute, and a single "pah" sound is made with the mouth. It happens so quickly that the movement is completed on a count of only one.

Figure 215

Figure 216

Figure 217

Figure 218

Working with a Partner

This exercise is probably one of the best "opening up" ways. If someone is standing there in an on-guard position, you can open him up instantly to get at his vital points in the neck before he has even realized it. Your partner again assumes an on-guard stance, and you take the same stance as for fa-jing ch'uan exercise no. 1. Your waist turns to your left as your right palm strikes to the inside of his right wrist to Neigwan (fig.

Fa-Jing Ch'uan Training Methods

131

218). This is the first set-up point. Your left palm now comes underneath your right wrist, flexed ready to take over the control of his right arm. Your left wrist flicks into his right Neigwan point as your right palm is moved to your right by the action of your waist turning to your right (fig. 219). Your right palm slams into the inside of his left wrist at Neigwan as you begin to step forward with your right foot (fig. 220). Place your right foot, and as the weight moves slightly onto it, your right shuto strikes into his St 9 point on the left side of his neck (fig. 221). Your waist now turns to your left, back to center. Again, your partner moves back, still holding his on-guard stance, and you perform the same exercise all the way down to the end of your training space. Your partner can do the same thing to you back to the other end. You then perform the whole thing on the reverse side. Remember that although I used many words to relay

Figure 219

Figure 220

this information, the whole exercise only takes a split second, and on a count of one, the waist just shakes violently and does not actually turn. To "turn" sort of says that the movement is done in a controlled manner, and this movement is actually explosive and completely out of control, so to speak.

FA-JING CH'UAN TRAINING METHOD NO. 3

The third of the fa-jing ch'uan exercises is also one of the most useful "opening" methods. The difference is that this one "opens" from the closed side. The definition of "open and closed" sides is as follows: if I attack someone, or he has attacked me and I have defended as in Figure 222, then I am on his "open side." Here, I have to be careful of his other hand, because I am within reach of both his hands. In Figure 223 I am on his "closed side," which means that I am a lot safer because he cannot get me with his other hand. (Although, when

Figure 221

Figure 222

Fa-Jing Ch'uan Training Methods

doing fa-jing ch'uan methods, it really makes no difference because they are so explosive that you are in and doing the work before your opponent even knows about it.)

To begin, you are standing in the same position as for the previous two exercises. Step forward with your right foot as your waist turns to your right. Your right backfist is thrust out to your right by the turning of your waist (fig. 224). Your waist snaps back to your left as your left foot is dragged forward naturally to make up the distance that was increased by your right step. As your waist turns to your left, your right tiger paw fist, snapping palm up, punches violently in an arc from your right to your left (fig. 225). As your waist turns back to your right, your right fist turns over to palm down and strikes to your right by the action of the waist (fig. 226). Notice that your left palm has controlled his right forearm from that second punch.

Figure 223

Figure 224

As with all of these exercises, you must practice up and down the training hall until your whole body moves in harmony. The feet move in accordance with what is happening, not because your have thought to move them. The waist shakes violently in accordance with what is happening, not because you are consciously turning your waist.

Working with a Partner

Figure 225

Again, your partner stands in an on-guard position in front of you, just out of your reach. He has his right fist forward (a right on-guard stance). As you step in, your waist turns to your right and your right backfist attacks to the outside of his right forearm, preferably at a point called Triple Warmer 8 (Tw 8), shown in Figure 227. Striking this point hard enough using your largest knuckle, as in the backfist, drains energy from the body and can cause knockout or even

Figure 226

death if the attacker has a

Fa-Jing Ch'uan Training Methods

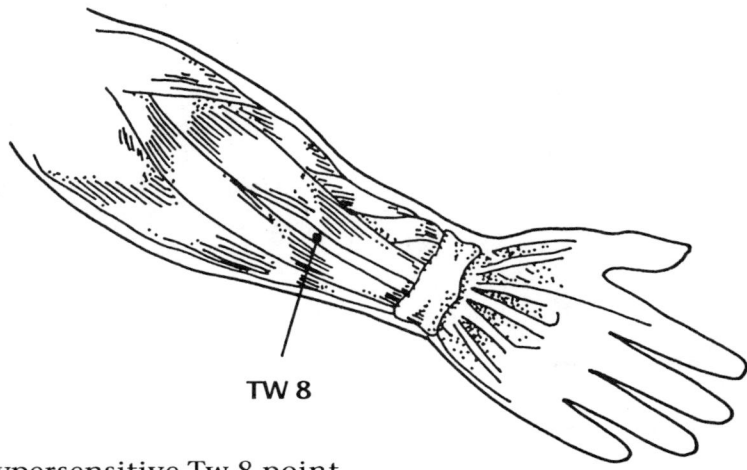

TW 8

hypersensitive Tw 8 point (fig. 228). (This point can simply be struck with a palm strike straight inward to cause KO.) Struck more lightly, it is an excellent set-up point for the very dangerous point strikes that follow. As your waist turns back to your left, your right fist turns palm up and strikes either to a point called Governor Vessel 26 (Gv 26) or to the Mind Point (fig. 229). The point that is struck depends on how hard your initial backfist is. If hard, it would turn his head so that you might not be able to strike Gv 26 with your tiger paw fist, so you would use the Mind Point.

Figure 227

Figure 228

Ultimate Dim-Mak: How to Fight a Grappler and Win

MIND POINT

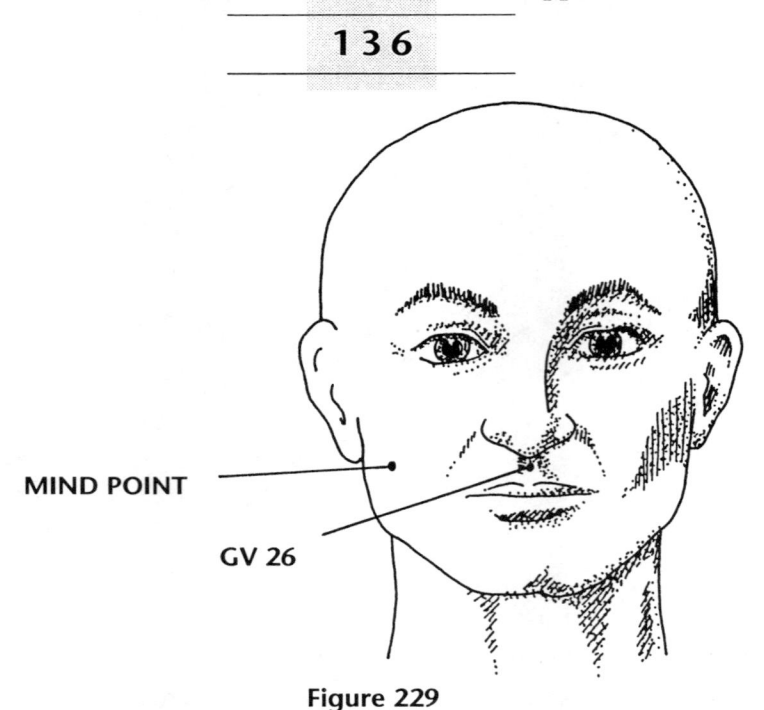

GV 26

Figure 229

Figure 230

The strike to Gv 26 causes death if struck hard and complete disorientation even when struck lightly (fig. 230). The strike to the Mind Point prevents the nerve signals from getting to the brain, and so he falls down (fig. 231). Notice that your left palm is now controlling his right forearm in both cases. Your waist turns back to your right, which causes your right fist to turn palm down and strike his right temple at Gall Bladder 3

(Gb 3), as in Figure 232. This point is, of course, a death point.

Again, you work up and down the training hall, and you also perform the exercise on the reverse side. This third exercise is the first one in which you can have your partner actually attack you with a right or left straight punch. Because you have to step in, there is no danger of your just standing there waiting for his attack to reach you when it is at full power. You must step in to intercept his attack. You may do this with all of these exercises, of course, but the movements must be totally subconscious and you must move in as he attacks. With the first two, there is the danger that you might just stand there and wait.

FA-JING CH'UAN TRAINING METHOD NO. 4

The fourth exercise also works on the closed side and begins with the backfist to Colon 10.

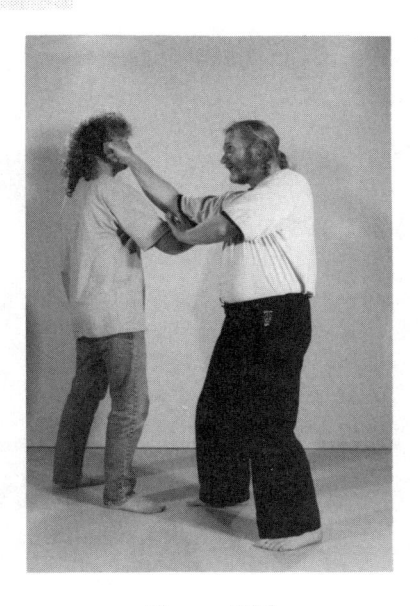

Figure 231

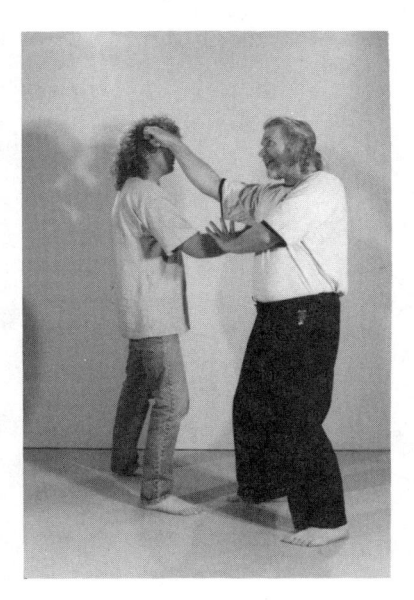

Figure 232

Standing in the beginning posture, you turn your waist to your right, which causes your right backfist to strike to your right (fig. 233). As your waist begins to turn back to your left, your left palm strikes just under your right forearm and you have taken a right step forward and slightly to your left (fig. 234). As your waist shakes back to your left fully, your right knife edge is thrust in and slightly downward (fig. 235). Note that the right knife edge is not actually pushed down but has a slightly downward motion as it is thrust forward. The main thrust is forward. Your left foot has shuffled forward also to keep the shoulder width stance. You now perform this fa-jing ch'uan up and down the dojo, until you know that you have the explosive power. Do it on the reverse side also. Simply doing these exercises will teach you to get the power.

Figure 233

Figure 234

Fa-Jing Ch'uan Training Methods
139

Working with a Partner
For this exercise you will learn about Stomach 11 (St 11) and Triple Warmer 8 (Tw 8). The location of St 11 is shown in Figure 236.

Figure 235

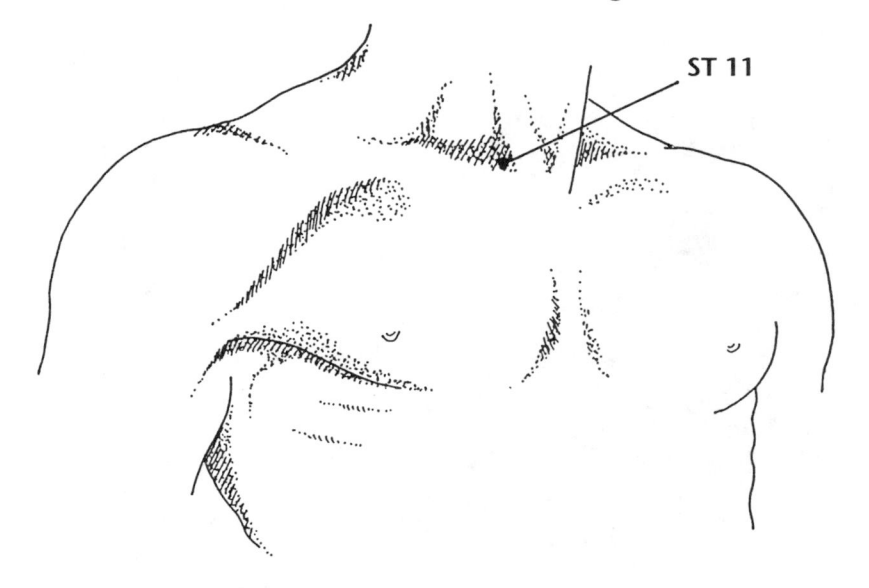

Figure 236

Ultimate Dim-Mak: How to Fight a Grappler and Win

Figure 237

Figure 238

Your partner is again standing in front of you holding an on-guard stance. Later he will be able to attack you with either a punch or a grappling type of movement where his right arm is coming forward to you. You shake your waist violently to your right as you strike his forearm at Tw 8 (fig. 237). As you step forward and slightly to your left, the momentum of your waist turning right causes your left palm to strike at Co 10 just as your waist is finishing the turn (fig. 238). As your waist shakes back to your left, your right knife edge, palm up, is thrust down and into St 11 just on top of the collarbone notch (fig. 239). This strike, especially when set up by the Tw 8 and Co 10 strikes, is devastating to the body. St 11 controls to some extent what the heart does. It changes the state of the heart (i.e., if he is awake, it will knock him out; if he is unconscious, it can be used as a revival point). It is also an extreme energy drainage point.

Fa-Jing Ch'uan Training Methods

Your partner takes a step back, and you perform this up and down the dojo on both sides. Again, this whole exercise has only taken a split second to perform and is done on a count of one.

FA-JING CH'UAN TRAINING METHOD NO. 5

The dim-mak points used in Explosive Energy Fist No. 5 are Gall Bladder 19 (Gb 19); Bladder 10 (Bl 10), or Neurological Shutdown (NS) point No. 3 (the old rabbit chop at the side of the back of the neck in a lateral line just slightly under the ear lobe); Gall Bladder 20 (Gb 20); and Triple Warmer 17 (Tw 17). The locations of these points are illustrated in Figures 240 through 243, respectively.

The gall bladder points used are knockout points, having much the same effect upon the carotid sinus that St 9 has. However, they also have physical implications because of

Figure 239

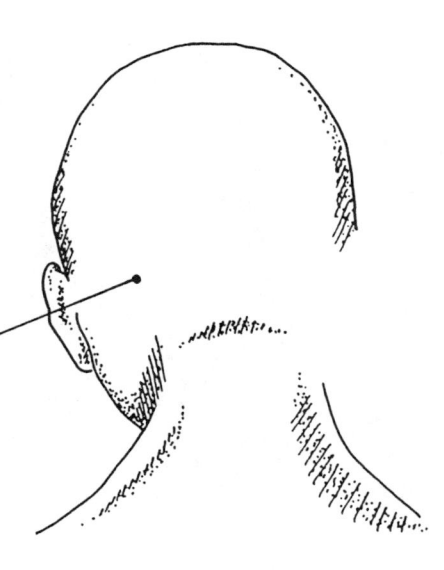

GB 19

Figure 240

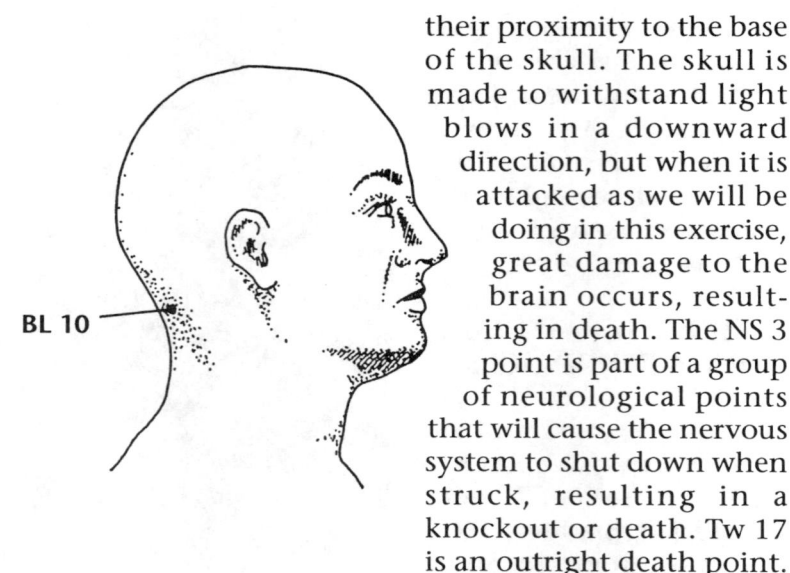

their proximity to the base of the skull. The skull is made to withstand light blows in a downward direction, but when it is attacked as we will be doing in this exercise, great damage to the brain occurs, resulting in death. The NS 3 point is part of a group of neurological points that will cause the nervous system to shut down when struck, resulting in a knockout or death. Tw 17 is an outright death point. When it is struck there is not much hope of revival.

This is the first of the explosive energy fist exercises for which we have to perform two fa-jing movements. The previous ones were all done in one fa-jing movement. Standing in the beginning position, turn your waist to your right and violently slam down to your right with your right palm (fig. 244). Your waist rebounds back to your left and then begins to turn right again as your

BL 10

Figure 241

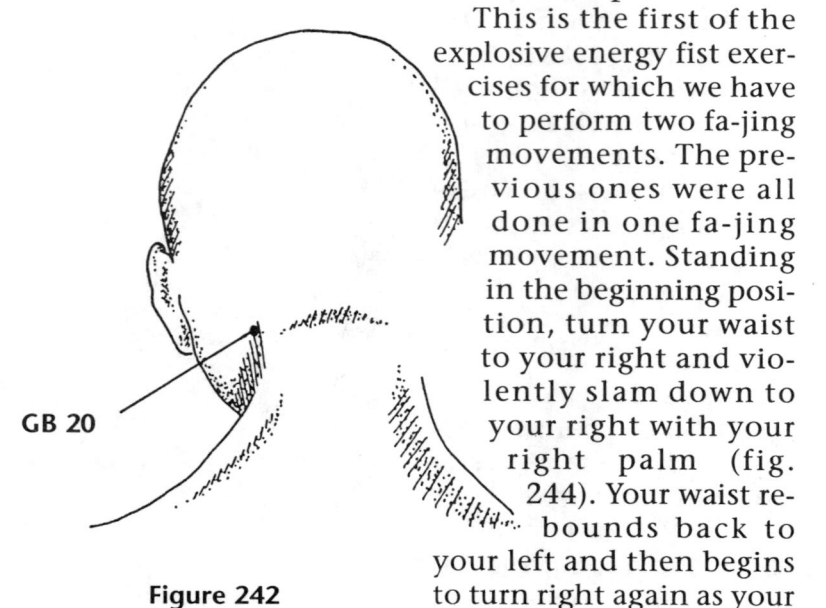

GB 20

Figure 242

Fa-Jing Ch'uan Training Methods

left palm slams down to your right, a little forward of where your right palm ended up (fig. 245). Your weight has also come forward onto your right foot slightly at this point. Take a left step forward as quickly as possible, maintaining perfect balance (fig. 246). Swivel on your heels, turning your body to the rear, so that your waist has turned to your right fully. As you do this, strike with your left palm straight ahead (fig. 247). As your waist turns violently back to your left, your right tiger paw fist strikes forward also (fig. 248). Your waist rebounds back to center. You are now in the same position except you are facing the opposite direction from where you started. You now perform the whole exercise beginning in the opposite direction. With this exercise, you do not move up and down the dojo, but rotate on a one-step area. When you wish to do this exercise on the opposite side, simply take a step forward with your

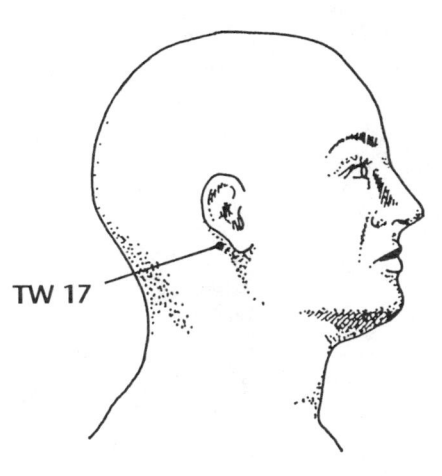

TW 17

Figure 243

Figure 244

left foot but stay facing the same direction; do not swivel.

Figure 245

Figure 246

Fa-Jing Ch'uan Training Methods

Figure 247

Figure 248

Working with a Partner

Your partner rushes at you and tries to go low to tackle you. Many grapplers use this method to great advantage against punchers and kickers, who are not used to this type of attack. You immediately slam your right palm down onto the back of his head at Gb 19 (Fig. 249). Your left palm slams down onto NS No. 3 (Gb 10), as your waist shakes to the left and then back to your right (fig. 250). Take a step forward, and as you swivel, your left palm will attack Gb 20 (fig. 251). Your waist has turned violently to your right at this point. As your waist turns to your left, your right tiger paw fist attacks to his Tw 17 point at the back of his right ear (fig. 252). Your partner now rushes at you from the opposite direction, and the whole exercise is repeated. Do it on the other side as well.

Figure 249

Figure 250

Fa-Jing Ch'uan Training Methods

147

Figure 251

Figure 252

Figure 253

Figure 254

FA JING CH'UAN TRAINING METHOD NO. 6

The dim-mak points that are used in this exercise are Gb 19, NS 3 or Gb 10, and the eyes.

From the beginning posture, shake your waist right, left, and right again. This takes only a split second. As you do this, both of your palms slam down onto your right knee. Time it so that you are doing the final turning of your waist to your right when the palms contact the knee (fig. 253). As soon as the knee touches the palms, it is thrust down onto the ground again, because you don't want to be left on one leg. Your waist now turns to your right for the second fa-jing movement, and your right palm scoops down to your right (fig. 254). As your waist violently shakes back to your left, your right fingers gouge up (fig. 255). Your waist now shakes back to your right as your left palm slams down (fig. 256). The last two moves, fingers and left palm,

Fa-Jing Ch'uan Training Methods

strike one after the other, very close together. Also do this on the reverse side.

Many fighters get into difficulty and are knocked off balance when someone tackles them. They just aren't used to this type of attack. Their balance and grounding are not sufficient to withstand this attack. To achieve proper balance and grounding, you have to do some sort of exercise, such as the "post" exercises presented in my book *Advanced Dim-Mak* and also on my video No. MTG54. This is especially important when standing on one leg. If you have not done these exercises, it is advisable not to lift one of your legs as in the above exercise.

Figure 255

Working with a Partner

Your partner again attacks you, first going high to put you off guard, and then going low as for the previous exercise. Both of your palms slam down onto his Gb 19 points at the back of his skull as your right knee lifts into his face. Your waist has

Figure 256

Ultimate Dim-Mak: How to Fight a Grappler and Win

150

done a fa-jing shake right, left, and right (fig. 257). It is not so much the knee that does the damage as the strikes to Gb 19. Your foot is placed quickly as your right palm slides around to his eyes with a right waist shake (fig. 258). As your waist shakes from left to right again, your right fingers gouge up into his eyes (fig. 259) and your left palm strikes down onto his NS 3 point at the back of his neck.

Figure 257

FA-JING CH'UAN TRAINING METHOD NO. 7

The dim-mak point used in this next training method is Gall Bladder 20 (Gb 20).

Standing with your right foot forward, turn your waist to your left violently, and your left elbow strikes down to your left side (fig. 260). Your waist shakes back to your right using the rebound from the previous movement, and then it shakes back to your left. Your left elbow again strikes down to your left, exactly the same as in

Figure 258

Figure 260. Your left foot now steps half a step to your rear and to what will become your left when you turn. As you turn your body to the rear, using the second shake of your waist, strike with your right palm straight ahead (fig. 261). As your waist shakes back to your right, your left palm follows (fig. 262).

Figure 259

Figure 260

Ultimate Dim-Mak: How to Fight a Grappler and Win

152

Figure 261

Figure 262

Fa-Jing Ch'uan Training Methods

Working with a Partner

Your partner attacks you suddenly, goes high to fool you, and then goes low to grab you just under your arms to try to take you down. This is a typical grappler's attack (fig. 263). Shake your waist using fa-jing and strike him with your left elbow to Gb 20 (fig. 264). Using the momentum gained from this first fa-jing shake, you again attack him using that same elbow to the same point on the back of the neck. His hold is greatly reduced by now, as he is either dead or knocked out, so step to your rear and slightly to what will become your left with your left foot and, twisting your whole body to the rear, strike him at Gb 20 with your right palm (fig. 265). As your waist shakes back to your right, your left palm strikes also to his Gb 20 point (fig. 266). This is death outright.

Figure 263

Figure 264

Ultimate Dim-Mak: How to Fight a Grappler and Win

154

Figure 265

Figure 266

FA-JING CH'UAN TRAINING METHOD NO. 8

In this training method you will be using two set-up points on the forearms, simply slapping both forearms down to St 9 and Cv 22.

With your right foot, take a right step forward, shake your waist to your left, and open both palms out to your sides and up slightly (fig. 267). As your waist begins to shake back to your right, your right palm lowers and then your left palm comes to the front and also lowers slightly (fig. 268). As your waist shakes back to your left, your right fingers poke forward with the thumb held in (fig. 269). Your waist rebounds to your right as your left fingers also poke forward (fig. 270.)

Figure 267

Figure 268

Ultimate Dim-Mak: How to Fight a Grappler and Win

156

Figure 269

Figure 270

Fa-Jing Ch'uan Training Methods

Working with a Partner

Your partner can either stand in his on-guard position or rush at you with both hands. I'll have him rushing at me this time. Remember to step up to meet him as he is coming forward. It's not good to allow him to be at full power when he gets to you. You step in with your right foot, opening up both arms (fig. 271) and turning your waist to your left. As you fa-jing shake back to your right, your right palm slams down onto the outside of his left forearm (setup), slamming it down and dragging it toward you (i.e., you slide your right palm down his left forearm, as in Figure 272). Immediately after this has been done and with the rebound of your waist to your right, your left palm now slams down onto his right forearm in exactly the same manner (fig. 273). As your waist shakes back to your left, the right thumb side of your right palm slams into St 9 point, causing knockout or death (fig. 274).

Figure 271

Figure 272

Ultimate Dim-Mak: How to Fight a Grappler and Win

158

Your waist again shakes back to your right, and your left fingers poke violently into the pit of his neck at Cv 22 (fig. 275). You must practice this method up and down the dojo and on both sides.

FA-JING CH'UAN TRAINING METHOD NO. 9

This next exercise exemplifies the coordination needed between the fa-jing shaking and what the hands are doing to the opponent. You will be learning about Stomach 10 point, or St 10. I have not spoken about St 10 before, so I will give a brief location. It is located halfway between St 9 and St 11 on the anterior border of the sternocleidomastoideus, that big muscle that runs up the sides of your neck (fig. 276). A straight-in strike to this point will cause the head to "explode." I do not mean this literally, of course, but it gives the head a feeling of being inflated to the point where it feels like it will explode

Figure 273

Figure 274

with energy and the person faints. It is one of the more dangerous points and will cause death from heart failure.

Figure 275

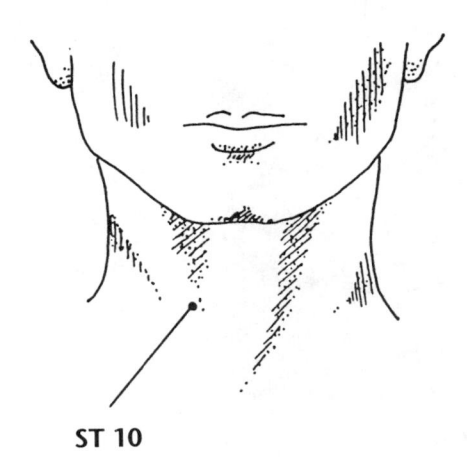

ST 10

Figure 276

From your starting position, shake your waist out to your left. Your palms will also be moved violently out to your left, the left one facing right while the right is facing left (fig. 277). As your waist shakes (rebounds) back to your right, your hands, remaining in their position, also shake violently to your right (fig. 278). You have also taken a right step forward as you make the first turn to your left. Now, as your waist rebounds to your left, thrust your right tiger paw fist forward (fig. 279). Practice this on both sides.

Figure 277

Figure 278

Figure 279

Working with a Partner

Again, you can use this as an "opening" method as your partner stands in an on-guard stance, or you can use it against a grappling type of rush in. Your partner rushes at you with both hands. You step forward to meet him as you slam both arms into his right forearm, shaking your waist to your left (fig. 280). With the rebound of your waist to your right, your palms immediately slam into his left forearm (fig. 281). As you shake back to your left, your right tiger paw fist strikes straight into St 10, causing KO or death (fig. 282).

Figure 280

Figure 281

Figure 282

ON STOMACH 10 POINT

R: Now, at this workshop, you have introduced St 10 as the big bad brother of St 9. I noticed many of the participants grabbing for their point location books when you talked about St 10. You spoke about many points, but St 10 really stuck in my mind. Is there a reason for this?

E: Yes, of course. I try to introduce at least one new point, something that people do not know about, at each workshop tour. Sure, I talk about many points, and we work on many different points, but the way that I introduced St 10 made it important, and it will stick in their minds now forever. In this way, I bring people up slowly, learning one important point each visit. The others they will remember simply because of learning the small san-sau; it will be in their bodies even if not in their minds. But the new point will be in both mind and body. It's a very dangerous point, not

Fa-Jing Ch'uan Training Methods

only because of its location but also because it is an "electrical" point as well as a physiological point.
R: Can you explain about these two types of points?
E: There are only two types of points, electrical and physical. The physical points are those that work the easiest, as they have under them some important physiological thing, like, for instance, the carotid sinus under St 9 or the heart right under Cv 14. These points work like a charm, as the person doesn't really feel any pain—he just wakes up (provided the strike was not too hard), not knowing how he got onto the ground. However, the energy or electrical points cause great pain as well as KO or death by disrupting the whole energy or qi system of the body. So when you hit a point that is both electrical and physiological, then you have a dangerous point indeed. St 10 is one of these points. It is found halfway between St 11 on the clavicle notch and St 9 and located right over the sternocleidomastoid muscle. It must be struck in at a shallow angle to have the best result. However, St 10 requires much more accuracy, and a smaller weapon must be used, like a tiger paw fist, where only one knuckle is used, or the tips of one finger. . . . So it takes a little more training to use these points, whereas the physical points require much less training to cause KO or death.

FA-JING CH'UAN TRAINING METHOD NO. 10

This next exercise is simpler than the previous ones; however, it is no less effective. It teaches us about using fa-jing as we shock the attacker's body and then attack to the same points twice in that split second of fa-jing shake. There are no particular points used in this method, as we are executing a neurological shutdown (although we do strike to a number of different points that collectively cause the shutdown).

From the starting position, take a right step forward

Figure 283

and turn your waist to your left, which causes your right backhand to be loaded (fig. 283). The waist shakes back to the right causing the right backhand to strike to your right as your left foot is dragged forward naturally to get back to the natural stance (fig. 284). Your waist now rebounds to your left, again loading the right palm. The waist again rebounds to your right, causing a second strike to the same position with your backhand. The whole thing has taken but a split second.

Figure 284

Working with a Partner

Your partner is in the on-guard position, or he attacks you. You move in to him as you turn your waist to your left. As in the previous method, both your right and left palms strike his right forearm (fig. 285). As your waist turns to your right, your right backhand strikes the side of his jaw (fig. 286). Your right backhand bounces back to the left and again strikes him on the right side of his jaw, encompassing the lower part of the ear (fig. 287). Figure 288 shows the positioning of the back of the palm on the side of his face. This alone causes a neurological shutdown. It must be a stinging, slapping movement, so the instant the palm strikes the face, it is withdrawn, ready for the next strike. Your waist rebounds to your left, and you withdraw both palms left. The waist rebounds to your right again, and both palms do the same strikes—the left to the forearm and the right

Figure 285

Figure 286

Ultimate Dim-Mak: How to Fight a Grappler and Win

166

backhand to the side of his face. You have done two similar strikes to the side of his face. The second strike, however, is a little lower on his face than the first. This ensures that you strike the whole area of NS 1.

• • •

The above 10 fa-jing ch'uan movements will give you all the fa-jing methods necessary to deal with a grappler or any type of attacker. Remember, it is not so much the "non-techniques" that you are learning, but rather the hidden areas, like body-mind coordination and the ability to counter any type of attack. You might combine some of these movements, or you might use less than what I have given in any situation. Practice is the key. The more of it you do, the more proficient you will be at dealing with attacks at a subconscious level.

Figure 287

Figure 288

CHAPTER

The Mind of the Grappler

FOUR

The very way that a grappler fights causes him to think differently than the more normal "punch/kick" martial artists. He is a stalker, constantly thinking of ways to cover that dangerous and vulnerable distance between himself and his prey. He is an attacker, not a defender. Grapplers do not learn grappling for self-defense; it is not a great self-defense method. Perhaps it could be used against one assailant, but against a number of attackers the grappler does not have very good tools at his disposal. He must come in close and grab his attacker, thereby leaving himself vulnerable to attack from others while he is busy fighting the first. So a grappler must be the attacker; he cannot afford to wait until someone attacks him.

Grapplers do very well in tournaments, where there are some rules and they are fighting one on one. In the ring, the grappler is able to stalk his victim, waiting for his chance to rush in and take him to ground, perhaps getting the choker on him and putting him to sleep or taking a submission hold to win the match.

In the street the grappler is also the attacker. As far as he is concerned, there is not much difference between fighting in the ring and fighting in the street. He shows all he has in the ring and brings only those weapons with him onto the streets. They are very good weapons, but that's all he has; nothing is hidden.

He waits and watches your every move, and he studies your body language. This is another reason grapplers do very well in tournaments against boxers and karateka. Why do karateka jump around in tournaments? They are actually taught to! They jump all over the place, letting the attacker (a grappler) know exactly how their bodies work: when they are at their most vulnerable and when it is not good to attack. By jumping around, we tell the opponent when we are about to attack and when it is good for him to attack us! Boxers make this mistake also. This is not good. You would not see a professional poker player smiling when he has a good hand, nor does he look sad when he has a rotten hand. He maintains a "poker face." (But then, tournaments would be quite uninteresting if the combatants just stood there waiting. I guess they must give the public something to look at.)

Since the grappler must get to you first, he is wary at first, knowing that this time his opponent just might know something and be able to take him out as he rushes in. So he stalks, watching how his opponent moves from side to side, watching to see how he raises his foot to move, how he places his weight when he is off guard and thinking about his movements, how he reacts to the audience or any distraction, and so on. Then he begins to put in little distractions to see how his opponent reacts to them. He raises his foot and pretends to kick to the legs—an ineffectual kick that would not hurt anyone. But the opponent reacts greatly to this kick, as he is used to fighting people who know how to kick. He moves backward when this kick is thrust forward, and at this point he is off guard.

Grapplers generally do not spend much time on

The Mind of the Grappler

their kicking or punching; therefore, their kicks in particular are not that great, so there is no reason for the boxer or the karateka to react to these little kicks. However, usually the boxer has heard about the great prowess that martial artists have in kicking, so he reacts violently in retreat when a totally ineffectual kick is put forward. The same is true with the karateka. He knows that a kick to the legs can damage him, so he reacts the same way. The grappler knows all of this; part of the craft of a good stalker is to know his prey. He knows about psychology, and he knows that the average martial artist has never been in a real fight. He knows that the only fighting most karate or kung fu martial artists have done has been in the safety of their dojo against their friends or teachers, who are aren't really going to hurt them. He knows that in such schools they use techniques that just don't work in the street or against a good grappler. He knows that the real stuff—the hidden training methods of the kung fu expert—has not been taught, because it has been forgotten, making kung fu totally ineffectual in the street. He also knows that any kung fu person who has been taught the inner meaning of his art would never enter a tournament. He knows that only the most basic of kung fu people—those with only minimal knowledge—would enter into these tournaments. The grappler does things in the ring to make his opponent move so that he can judge how he moves and why. He throws out a couple of ineffectual kicks or perhaps a couple of well-out-of-range punches, makes a few sudden moves from left to right, stamps his foot, or moves in. He doesn't attack just yet, because he is still working out how the opponent is going to react to the real attack. The opponent, if he knows his craft, will not react. He will have the "poker face," knowing when the real attack is coming or if a movement is a feint.

This is important because this is where part of the defense against a grappler comes in. A feint is exactly the same as an attack in the attacker's mind. He has to go through all of the same mind games and body movement to perform the feint, expecting the other person to react in the same way all of his opponents have: to move back and become tense. The grappler, like any person, has internal "switches" in his brain. The grappler's switches have been trained to switch on when certain things happen. He knows that a person will react the same way every time he does something, like throwing out that ineffectual kick. The opponent's reaction, or movement, is the switch that tells the grappler when to attack and how. If, however, the opponent does not react at all to this false attack, then no switches turn on in the grappler's brain and he becomes confused. And if the opponent reacts in a completely opposite manner, for instance, coming forward and attacking the grappler with great ferocity, like a wild animal and not some helpless human being, the grappler is even more confused. He is used to people being defensive and not offensive, so his switches are not turned on.

It is the same in real self-defense, when we are attacked for real. An attacker in the street is usually streetwise and has learned many "switches" in his life. If those switches are not turned on, then he becomes confused and, more often than not, runs away.

THE FEINT

The grappler has many different feints in his bag of tricks. He is trying you out at this stage, to see what you will do. There are two possible responses to a feint, and which one you use depends the proximity to your attacker. If the attacker feints when he is well out of your field of striking, you do not move, you do not react, and you do not let him "know you." If, however, the feint is within your field of striking, you attack with great speed and power. This takes the opponent totally off guard and puts you in the driver's seat. His mind has not attacked; only his body has made some pretend movement. But in doing this, his body has had to sort of start and stop. It is during this time that you attack. He is not ready for this, and the switch that his mind is waiting for is not turned on. Instantly, he has to force himself to find another switch. But it is not there because he is not used to someone doing this to him, to attacking him as he feints.

He might throw up an arm, expecting you to get ready to block or to move back (fig. 289). If he is within range, you rush at him, simultaneously taking out his raised arm and striking him in the neck at St 9 point (fig. 290). Remember your awareness training, and move

Figure 289

Figure 290

at the same time as he does if he is within range.

The "silly little kick" is often used by the grappler to test what you will do or to cause you to back off. As you back off, he rushes at you in an attempt to surprise you.

Again, if his kick is within striking range, you must rush *forward*, not back. Even if the kick touches you, it will not be powerful; he is using it as a testing device, and most grapplers are not good kickers anyway. Test yourself. Take a few kicks to your midsection; attack your partner with your belly, pushing out your abdomen and breathing out. You will be surprised at how quickly you will be able to take kicks to the belly.

The very instant he attacks with a feint kick, you must attack him. Rush in, slamming his leg at the knee (fig. 291). Try to take his kneecap off with your palm strike. He will have only one foot on the ground at this point and will be totally confused, as you have not

Figure 291

Figure 292

The Mind of the Grappler

done what he is expecting. So now you keep on attacking with your hands, perhaps a shuto to his neck (fig. 292).

Or from bagwa we have the following. Your attacker executes a front kick (this is the one used by most grapplers, because it is easy and requires less training than other, more strenuous kicks), your right palm slams his right knee, as in Figure 293. You then grab his leg with your right palm, turning your body to your right and stepping in close to his body and lifting his leg (fig. 294). Now your left palm can slam down onto his genitals (fig. 295).

It is important for any martial artist to know exactly how the grappler thinks so he can combat him. Remember the classic Chinese saying: "To know his mind is to know how he moves."

Figure 293

Figure 294

Figure 295

CHAPTER

Fighting Methods

FIVE

The neck is the most vulnerable place on the human body. We have protective reflex actions for the eyes and groin, but no such reflex action for the neck. And because it connects your head and body, it can be targeted to great effect in self-defense, especially against grapplers. As you may have noticed in my previous chapters, almost all my training methods are devoted to the neck. In a tight situation, attacking the neck will never let you down.

The same is not true for sports martial arts, though. Too many people nowadays are not distinguishing between sports and self-defense. So, when we make a sport from a very deadly self-defense system, people are hurt or killed in the ring. It is my view that you take up karate or kung fu either for the sport of it or to defend yourself, and never the two should meet. If you practice to enter into tournaments to find out how good you are, there is the real possibility that you will use that form of sport when you are attacked in the street and lose—perhaps your life. On the other hand, if you only practice for deadly self-defense and then enter into a competition, there is the risk of using some deadly strikes that have become reflex actions because of your self-defense training, and finding someone dead at your feet.

If you do tournament karate, train for it; if you do karate for self-defense, then train for it. Do not allow the two to mix. Sports karate is great—it provides an outlet for those who are interested in combative sports other than football, and it's safer than football. However, if you are one of those who has taken up the martial arts for self-defense and do not wish to get decked in your first street confrontation, as so many black belts do, you need to know where to strike, rather than just hitting your opponent in the face or belly. There are some pretty tough lads out there—lads who have had more real fights than most black belts and know how to take a punch. They have the added advantage of never having trained in the dojo in unrealistic situations, so the only fighting they know and are accustomed to is that which is real.

A martial artist is not necessarily a fighter or good at self-defense. People make the mistake of thinking that they will become good at self-defense just because they join their local karate or kung fu club. The martial artist must know how to turn his art into a self-defense method; what we learn in the dojo only gives us the tools to learn self-defense.

ON USING TECHNIQUE FOR SELF-DEFENSE

R: You began your workshop here by saying something like "form or kata and point theory just isn't enough to learn self-defense. " Can you elaborate on this?

E: Okay, just think for a minute logically. A person comes to a martial arts class and learns kata and bunkai, and does some sparring. What has he learned? Just that— logical physical movement. He is the same person at the end of his training as he was before he started. He knows some points and has worked out what each movement in his kata means, tuite-wise, but he still isbeaten in the street; he doesn't get a chance to use his fancy techniques or point strikes. Why? Because he hasn't taken his martial art into the realm of a self-defense system. And to do this it must become internal, or reflex. And the only way to cause a martial art to go internal is by training in the "training methods" of the internal systems. These cause simple things like putting our hands up in front of our faces when attacked, a yin response, to become a yang response. We turn that movement into a devastating attack to vital points. So now, the person who began karate of taiji years ago has reflex actions that are self-defense actions and not just cover-up actions.

R: But surely, years of bunkai and kata training have their place?

E: Sure, that is where we learn about coordination and timing, without which our self-defense art would be nothing more than brawling, where the strongest person wins. Think of it this way: the martial arts are logical. We move in a certain pattern; this is logical. We use certain techniques against certain attacks; this is also logical. A street attacker does not fight logically, and you cannot fight an illogical attack using a logical defense. The two just don't mix. So we need an illogical method of fighting to defend ourselves. Reflex actions are illogical, they just happen; we do not "think" about them using our conscious brain, so they are illogical. We use the training methods such as "small san-sau," which we covered at this workshop, to train our body and mind in reflex defensive actions.

R: The "small san-sau." Can you elaborate on the reason for doing it and where it came from?

E: The reason is that it is the best training method for all martial artists to train in, regardless of style, to turn their logical martial art into an illogical self-defense art. Physically, it gives mind/body coordination, [it gives] power over short distances, it shows where to hit without even looking, it gives the correct direction without even knowing, and it gives the set-up points without having to think about them.

R: But isn't this what we get from practicing techniques?

E: No, what you get from practicing technique is coordination, but you also get a negative, in that techniques are logical—he attacks here, and I do this, etc. Small san-sau teaches us about nontechnique. Yes, we are learning techniques, but the overall thing that we get from this is that when attacked, the body will just react; we do not have to think about any technique. You will do whatever is necessary, depending upon what the opponent is doing to you, and not try to do some technique regardless of what is happening to you. This ensures that when attacked, we rely subconsciously on what is happening to us to dictate what we do back to him. So his movement causes our body to move automatically with the correct response, quickly and without thinking. It is said, that small san-sau covers all known attacks, and so we learn about all known defenses subconsciously. Learning only techniques tells us that we must think about doing a certain technique before his attack has happened, and it might be the wrong technique for that particular attack. Where [san-sau] came from? Well, it is my belief that Yang Sau-chung, the eldest son of Yang Cheng-fu, invented it, but I cannot be sure of this. I have found record of it only back to Sau-chung.

One second and you're dead. That's all it takes to knife you, shoot you, or strike your head with a baseball bat. Therefore, you learn to use the most deadly strikes possible, and then you make them reflex. For instance, when something is thrust toward your eyes, you almost always dodge the object by turning your head automatically, even though you haven't even seen it. Or when anything comes toward the crown jewels, you always flinch. The easiest way to turn a martial art into a self-defense system is to simply take all of those movements from your katas or training methods that are natural to the body and train in them. You do not train in any movements that are unnatural. You have to be able to react without thinking, so your hands must be able to move from the position that they are in, and not have to be changed to some other position first. Take the old reverse punch (fig. 296). It can never be made to be reflex because it is not a natural movement. The punch itself has to be brought right from the hip, which gives physical power but is slow, giving the grappler time to avoid it and take you to the ground. Punches like this have to be long; this is the only way to gain the necessary power. The body is low; the stance is low; the blocking arm has had to move into a tense, unnatural position; and the punch itself has to be "done" (i.e., the user has to think about it). There are too many movements involved for it to be a reflex action.

Figure 296

You have to be able to attack from any normal position, rather than having to take a deep stance. Therefore, your self-defense training is done from a natural stance, one that you might find yourself in at any time, such as in Figure 297. This stance is one of many that you could use and still be perfectly safe and on guard in a potentially dangerous situation. You are attacked, so your arms simply move outward as they would in a normal reflex action when you are startled suddenly (fig. 298). This also has a by-product. There is nothing worse than being in a situation that could have been calmed by just talking and your exacerbating it by taking the low, on-guard stance to show the attacker that you do karate or kung-fu. In many cases, the attacker will become even more aggressive if you try to scare him with a karate stance. And in more cases than not, he will beat you because you have trained in martial arts and not fighting.

The katas and forms have their place, of course, not so much to teach technique, but rather to teach timing, balance, and coordination. The big mistake people make when fighting for real is that they think that the techniques they learn in the katas are how they should fight! Katas and forms are logical; fights do not happen

Figure 297

Figure 298

logically. They are totally illogical, so we must use methods of self-defense that are not learned logically.

All martial artists have a couple of favorite movements, those that they use all the time and that work for them to some degree. Perhaps those movements are more natural to their particular body shape, for example. Right from the beginning of your training, it is important to learn movements that are going to be of the greatest help in a real life-or-death situation. This cannot be done, of course, if you are going to use your martial art for sport. In fact, it will be detrimental to your sport if you do train your mind and body to have deadly reflex actions. This would leave you with no automatic actions that you could use in the tournament, and you would have to be continually checking your deadly reflex action. As a result, you would gradually lose the self-defense reflex action, and then you are left with nothing—no sports or self-defense reflexes. Hence my earlier statement that sport is sport and self-defense is self-defense, and never the two should meet.

So we aim for anywhere on the neck. There are just so many things in the neck that will cause death or, at the the very least immobilization, that it is not necessary to even know the deadly points. You strike anywhere, and you will get something. By simply raising your arms against the old haymaker—just raising them, nothing special, no martial technique—you will almost always get the carotid sinus or St 9 point

Figure 299

Ultimate Dim-Mak: How to Fight a Grappler and Win

182

Figure 300

Figure 301

(fig. 299). This has only to be struck with a blow that any 6-year-old child can deliver to cause a KO by the action of the carotid sinus on the cardioinhibitory center in the brain, as described earlier.

Children are able to defend themselves using the neck as the striking area. All of my children know about the most deadly strikes to the neck (I can do this because they are home-schooled!). Because they know about the dangers, though, they are all quite responsible. All have had the pleasure of knocking Daddy out at least once just to show them that they can do it with ease.

A jabbing finger is a completely natural movement; we point subconsciously. So again, rather than placing your hands over your face in reaction to an attack, you simply raise your arms and poke the fingers into Cv 22. This causes death at most, or a coughing fit on the ground at least (fig. 300).

As shown in Figure 301,

Fighting Methods

simply moving to the side and throwing your arms outward blocks his straight punch. You should simultaneously attack to Small Intestine 16 (Si 16), another knockout or death point (fig. 302).

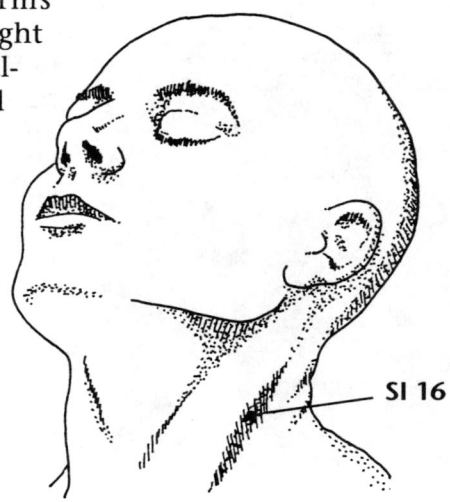

Figure 302

Ultimate Dim-Mak: How to Fight a Grappler and Win

Figure 303

Figure 304

All of the above methods can be used against grappling techniques. In fact, that is why we use these techniques: grapplers are the most dangerous of all fighters because they do things that we as "kick/punch" martial artists are not used to, so they are able to get in where most of us would not be able to. Once inside our defense, the grappler has at his disposal an arsenal of very dangerous locks and holds that can render anyone unconscious in seconds. So if a grappler rushes at you, raise your palms, at the very least, or use a devastating, powerful strike using the power of your waist to strike to his neck (fig. 303).

The back of the neck is not immune either. Just a light tap to one of the points located there can knock someone down and out. NS point No. 3 is on either side of the backbone in the neck and about halfway between the base of the skull and the shoulders. We strike it at a 180-degree angle to cause instant knockout or death. So if a grappler has rushed at you high, then goes low to surprise you, as many do, your palms simply thrust downward (fig. 304). We subconsciously do this downward movement many times during our day, so it is not a big thing to train the mind and body to react to such an attack instantly and without even thinking.

The last thing you want to do is to go to the ground, especially with a seasoned grappler. This is his territory, not yours. Again, use the tools from your own martial art to fight against a grappler; *do not try to grapple a grappler.* Nor should you take up grappling. No matter how hard you train, you will never reach the ability of the person who has been grappling all of his life. You have been training in kicking and punching, so you use what you have been training in, working it so that it is effective against a grappler. There is something drastically wrong with either your martial art or your ability if you cannot use it to fight a grappler. And if you have to use some grappling, do not do it when he is alert and strong. Slam him in the neck first (fig. 305), and then take him around the neck, making sure that your palm is hooked under his chin so that you are able to turn this hold into a sleeper hold (fig. 306). If he is still alert, and he tries to attack you with one of his other hands to the groin, for instance, violently shake his head; his

Figure 305

Figure 306

Figure 307

arms will flop and be useless (fig. 307).

The bottom line is, if in trouble, hit the neck. If not really in trouble, use martial arts techniques so that you do not go to gaol (jail) for excessive force. (I had one chap recently tell me that perhaps I should not tell police officers to use these deadly techniques. I told him that I had many students in the force, and that it is better to be alive and face a lawsuit than play it safe and be dead.)

THE METHODS OF GRAPPLER FIGHTING

The grappler will be on you before you even know about it. You blink or look sideways at something that distracts you, and you are gone. He is taking you down, and you are unable to do anything about it. You have trained using a kick bag for years, you can kick at 90 miles per hour, you can break 10 house tiles, and still you are taken down and beaten. How can this be? Because as a martial artist, you have only learned technique. This is fine when you only enter tournaments where the styles of fighting are basically the same, kicking and punching. Your "technique oriented" martial arts training works just fine against others with similar training. But against a stylist who is not oriented toward technique, you have had it. It's a bit like a boxer who only trains and fights against orthodox stances and fighters, and then he goes against his first southpaw and he is confused.

So the first thing your teacher must do is to train you to defend against all types of fighters and in as realistic a way as possible. And if your teacher cannot get in to take you down, then he should employ someone who can. Because as sure as eggs, a good grappler will be able to get in quickly behind your guard and take you down.

Danger time is measured in the distance between you and him. If you do not react instantly the moment your opponent moves, you have had it. And if you just stand there waiting for him to move on you, you have also had it. Even if your movement is subconscious or reflexive and you just stand there waiting, you still lose. The fine line of defense that we have against a grappler is our being trained to move forward the moment we are attacked. You will notice that all of the previously discussed training methods (bar those that are designed to train you to correct for mistakes where you haven't moved in) employ this. This method of defense is effective regardless of whether you are fighting a grappler or someone who has trained in some other kick/punch style. Either way, you will confuse the attacker by doing something he does not expect. By moving in, you upset his "switches," throwing off his timing and his power. If you also attack him as you do this, he is really up the creek as far as control is concerned. He is no longer in control of the situation; you are, and grapplers do not like to be in control.

You must become an animal, and there is a wonderful training method to explain this principle. It is one that I have derived from juggling, and it represents those martial artists who just wait until the attacker moves in on them, as well as those who do the right thing and attack the attacker. My little lad Ben was learning how to juggle (a great training method for the martial arts, by the way), and I was trying to invent training methods for him. One such training method was to simply throw balls to each other, so that we were catching both balls simultaneously. The first thing I noticed was that if we tried to focus on the balls, we missed at least one of them. So we decided that we would have to use the old "eagle vision" (a sort of peripheral vision). This was better, but each of us dropped at least one ball sometimes. So, I decided that we should use the old "reptile brain," and go out to attack the balls (excuse the pun). We had been allowing the balls to just come to us, so we now stretched our fingers and rounded our backs to get into a reptile brain mode, and when the balls came at us, we went out and attacked them with great power and energy. This worked every time.

The first method of waiting for the ball to come to us is analogous to the person who waits for the attacker to come to him. The second way, when we pursued the balls, represented the defender going out to attack the attacker.

Fighting against a grappler depends upon your fighting like an animal. A dog never thinks about fighting; it just goes out to the attacker and almost always tries to take the neck. Animals know instinctively that the neck is vulnerable.

The methods you use against a grappler depend upon what he is doing to you. The following exercises represent some situations that you might find yourself in. For the most part, I will be presenting those situations where you have done the right thing by going forward to intercept the attack with one of your own. However, I will demonstrate a few techniques that you can use to get out of a grappling situation where the attacker has been able to grab you because you have not done the right thing.

Years ago, when asked about certain jujutsu experts, James DeMille, a very tough jeet kune do expert, said that he would simply punch them before they got to him. And he was correct. Many martial artists of the kick/punch styles seem to forget all about their years of training in kicking and punching when attacked by a grappler. They do not even attempt to punch.

The first defense against a grappler is the most basic: simply punch him in the face as he attacks you (fig. 308). You do not have to strike any particular points at this stage, as long as your punch can be delivered from six inches away and at the very instant that he moves at you. Just aim for the face somewhere, perhaps the nose or the side of the jaw. Remember, though, that you must move in by taking a short step toward him as he attacks. The rear foot is also dragged forward as you do this. This is, in fact, doing what Bruce Lee said to do: "intercept the attack" before it gets to you—preempt it.

Figure 308

ON THE VALUE OF OTHER ARTS

R: In all of your workshops, you always make mention of other martial artists that you consider to have something. This I find refreshing, as these people could be considered to be your opposition.

E: There is no opposition in this business (well, I shouldn't call it a business; it's a way of life). The more good people there are out there, teaching good methods with a genuine love for their students, then the better place this world will be. If I can help someone else to be recognized in the USA, for example, then I will let all of my people know about these people, like Ken Johnson, who has a series of videotapes teaching sanchin kata in the correct way, which, to most people looks rather radical. But Ken is doing a lot of good out there and so should be recognized. Same when I go to Europe—I tell people there about others in the USA who are also doing good research themselves and not just sitting back and nodding to everything their sensei has told them. And I have always said, beg, borrow, buy, or steal the good info, no matter where it is found. So I will readily admit that I learn from everyone.

Figure 309

You should, of course, never give a sucker an even break, and so you should continue the attack using fa-jing type attacks that rebounded naturally from the first. For instance, from your first punch to the face, you might, as your waist returns to your right, attack with your left palm (fig. 309). This is a natural strike, because you have not had to reload first. The previous strike automatically "loaded" your left palm for another attack. This strike, in turn, auto-

Fighting Methods

matically loads the right elbow, and you strike again as your waist turned back to the left (fig. 310). You could keep going, but those three strikes are enough to put the toughest of fighters down. Again, we have not tried to use any specific points, just the face or the neck. Remember that if you strike the neck with an elbow, you are going to kill the attacker!

If you wanted to be a little more accurate and do some real damage, you might use the following methods against the same attack.

Instead of the simple face punch, you could use the tiger paw fist to attack his Cv 22 point (fig. 311). Following up and using the rebound from the first strike, you could come straight in with your elbow to just under the collarbone to attack to Stomach 12 (St 12; see fig. 312 for its exact location). Your waist turns to your left for the initial strike and then back to your right, which loads your right elbow for the strike

Figure 310

Figure 311

ST 12

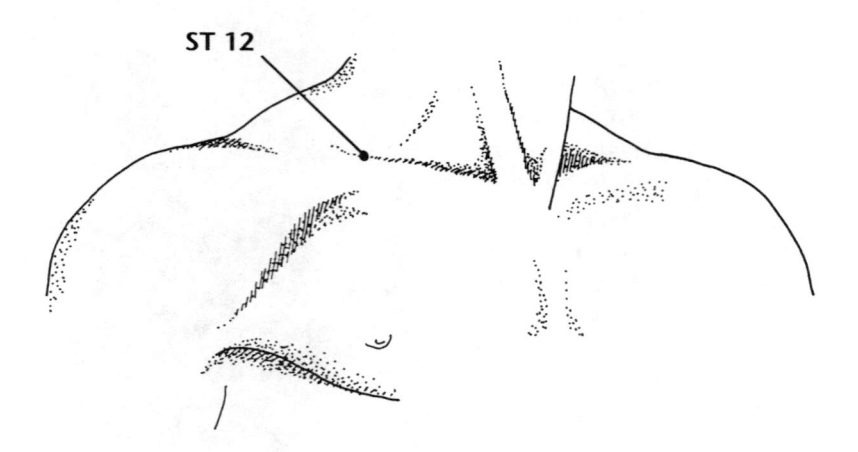

Figure 312

Figure 313

shown in Figure 313. St 12 point is said to take the will to fight away, and having had this point worked upon myself, I can tell you that it works. You just want to sit down or lie down when struck. Note that the elbow should be aimed in an upward direction into the lower side of the clavicle (collarbone) this time and not downward to the top of it. Continuing, as your waist shakes violently back to your right, rebounding from the elbow strike, your right shuto strikes into Si 16 (fig. 314).

Fighting Methods

193

A strike here causes his head to be "disconnected from his body" (not physically, but energywise). It is an extreme point and is only used in extremely dangerous situations. This attack takes only about one second.

For this next situation, we make use of the human phenomenon of neurological shutdown. A stinging/slapping strike to NS 2 causes the person to black out by the action of the brain on the whole nervous system. Just a bit of the lower part of the ear is struck, along with the lower line of the jaw. This strike also takes in important dim-mak points, such as TW 17 and Small Intestine 17 (Si 17), shown in Figure 315.

Figure 314

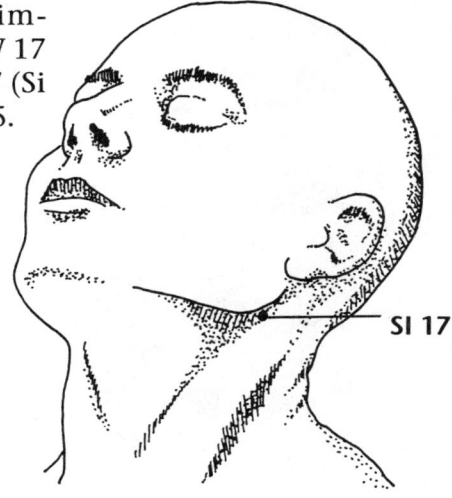

Figure 315

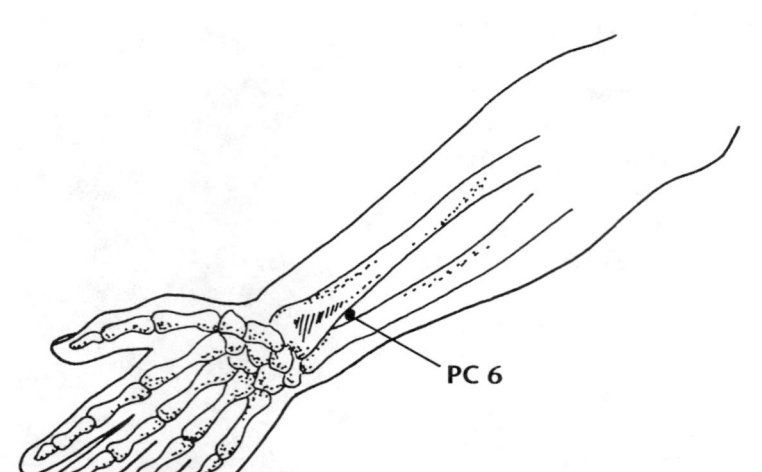

Figure 316

Figure 317

This time the grappler might attack with a more conventional grappling-type attack, by simply rushing at you with both hands coming at your upper body or face and neck. Strike his right arm with both your palms, the left striking to Neigwan (fig. 316) while the right palm strikes the inside of his elbow joint (fig. 317). Do not worry about his left arm, because the pain caused by the nerve strike to the elbow will probably put him down anyway, and the strike to Pc 6 will set up the NS 3 strike. Your waist has turned to your left to do this strike, so now it turns back to your right, taking

Fighting Methods

195

with it your right backhand to strike him at NS 2 (fig. 318), thus effecting the neurological shutdown.

Suppose the attacker has come at you high and then gone low, catching you before you have time to react. If your arms are caught, your hands should poke up into Cv 22 (fig. 319). If he has come underneath your on-guard arms, you can strike him on the back of his skull as well as the front of his skull (forehead) simultaneously, as in Figure 320. This causes a shock to the brain, which shuts down all bodily functions, thus causing a KO.

Figure 318

Figure 319

Ultimate Dim-Mak: How to Fight a Grappler and Win

If the worst-case scenario has occurred and he has been able to get behind you because you haven't done your anti-grappler training, immediately shake your waist violently to the rear and strike him with your elbow to the temple (Gb 3), as in Figure 321. This will cause him to let go and probably kill him, but just in case it hasn't, turn around quickly and take his head with your right (or left, as the case may be) arm and slip it around his neck, turning it laterally. A slight bend backward and you have a broken neck (fig. 322).

Triple Warmer 17 is one of the most dangerous points when struck from rear to front. Normally this is not easy to do, as most conventional martial arts require that you get behind the attacker first. However, from the dim-mak katas, we have a way of getting to this point from the front.

As you are being attacked, either by a right straight or a grabbing motion, move to your left

Figure 320

Figure 321

Fighting Methods

197

with your left foot as your left palm slams his right elbow (fig. 323). Notice the position of the right palm coming up underneath the left. As your waist is turning to your left (a reverse action, as you are striking to your right), the heel of your right palm strikes into the back of his ear to Tw 17 (fig. 324). The direction is correct because of the movement of your right palm swinging from your front to your rear

The whole movement takes only a split second. Be sure that you wish to kill the attacker when using this strike. However, just in case it has not done its job (perhaps you have missed Tw 17), you can now perform the second part of this movement. Your left palm pushes his right arm underneath your right arm as your right palm snakes around his neck, pulling him in (fig. 325). Your right palm now completes its travel, locking his neck (fig. 326). Only a small movement upward is enough to break the neck.

Figure 322

Figure 323

Ultimate Dim-Mak: How to Fight a Grappler and Win

198

Figure 324

Figure 325

Fighting Methods

199

Figure 326

SOME OTHER METHODS

Your assailant attacks with something to your face. You move to the outside of his right arm and "slip block" his right arm up the outside of his arm (set-up) with your left palm, which ends up striking to his temple, or Gb 3 (fig. 327). Your left palm immediately gouges around into his eyes as your left foot kicks to the back of his right knee at Kidney 10 (fig. 328). The initial strike will kill him if

Figure 327

done hard enough, but just in case it doesn't, then the follow-up methods will ensure victory.

You are attacked with the typical grappler's rush, both arms outward toward your body. Your left palm slams down into the crease of his right elbow, taking out his arm. Your right hammer fist strikes into the side of his neck, killing him (fig. 329). Your right palm snakes around the front of his neck and continues until you have him in the neck breaker (fig. 330). Your left palm is free to attack again to the neck or face.

The attacker comes in again with both arms. You step in to him, attacking with both of your tiger paw fists to the Gall Bladder 24 points, which are about two inches below the pectoral crease, directly in line with the nipples. This causes death or KO (fig. 331). Continue this line of attack by using the rebound from the previous attack, to attack the top of his neck where it joins the jawbone using both knife

Figure 328

Figure 329

Fighting Methods

201

edges of both hands (fig. 332). Be sure that the attack is for real before you use this method.

Figure 330

Figure 331

Ultimate Dim-Mak: How to Fight a Grappler and Win

Figure 332

Figure 333

Immediately move to either side as he attacks with both hands. If you moved to your left, your left hand will strike his right forearm, moving it to your right. Your right tiger paw fist strikes straight into his temple (fig. 333). Immediately pull him in and take a sleeper hold (fig. 334). When executing a sleeper hold of any kind, you must be sure that you have squeezed both sides of the neck, thus stopping all blood flow to the head.

The above methods,

plus those I have given in the rest of this book, will give you more than enough "techniques" to last a lifetime. However, as I keep stressing, it is not the techniques that are important, but rather the way we treat grappling-type attacks. You must get out of the habit if thinking fights last a long time, like in tournament fighting. They don't. The fight will be over in, at the most, 30 seconds, provided you have done your work. So you will notice that all of the ways of fighting that I have presented in this book are very deadly one- and two-movement attacks aimed at very deadly points on the human body. This will ensure your safety if ever you are attacked by anyone—grappler, kicker/puncher, or street fighter.

NOTE: My videos *How to Fight a Grappler, Vols. 1 & 2* show many of the methods presented in this book. For more information, contact MTG Publishing, P.O. Box 792, Murwillumbah NSW 2484, Australia; Fax: 61-66-797028.

Figure 334

CHAPTER

The Sleeper Holds

SIX

As I have already said, the neck is the most vulnerable area of the human body. There are no automatic defenses for the neck as there are for the groin or eyes. So in this section I will be covering some of the neck holds that will cause a person to black out within seconds of your applying the lock. These locks are called a number of different names, such as "sleeper hold," "choke out," "choker," and "blood KO."

In my earlier wrestling days (before professional wrestling became too silly), I saw people like Mark Lewin perform new and exotic moves, such as the sleeper hold. This involved taking a lock around the neck and squeezing it on both sides until the flow of blood to the brain stopped. The person would go to sleep in a matter of seconds. It was usually applied from the rear by folding the arms around the neck and head. However, there are a number of other ways to apply the old sleeper hold. Of course, you have to be able to get in there first. My advice, as always, is that you should never try to get any hold or lock on an attacker while he is fully awake. Stun him first with a point strike, and then get the lock on. This is the only way that locks will work in a realistic situation.

I use five sleeper holds—four standing up and one on the ground or against a wall. They are all equally quick.

FROM THE FRONT

Someone attacks with both hands from the front, as in a typical wrestler's or grappler's type of attack (fig. 335). I should move in as he attacks, slamming the inside of his right forearm at Neigwan (fig. 336). My right hand could also be blocking his left arm either from the outside or from the inside (figs. 337 and 338). My left palm, using a ricochet from his right forearm, immediately slams into his St 9 point on the right side of his neck (fig. 339), thus stunning him or knocking him out, making the next attack redundant anyway! The sleeper is locked in by my taking the radius side of my left forearm across his right carotid artery while I thrust my right ulna into his left carotid artery, thus block-

Figure 335

Figure 336

ing the supply of blood to his brain (fig. 340). My forearms have made a "V" shape across his neck, and my wrists have bent around the back of his neck to prevent him from escaping. All I have to do now is flex my arm muscles, and the pressure across his carotid is increased.

People often say to me that I am vulnerable while in this position because I am in front of the attacker. Keep in mind that he has been stunned by the first attack to St 9. And even if he is still awake and tries to strike my groin, I do not just stand there applying pressure; I rip his head off by shaking violently from side to side. This has never failed to stop any counterattack.

Figure 337

Figure 338

Figure 339

Figure 340

FROM BEHIND OR THE SIDE

The assailant again attacks. Again, I stun him with a shot to his St 9 point (fig. 341). This time, I take his neck with my right palm and his shoulder with my left (fig. 342). I quickly step to his right-hand side, pulling his body around as I do so (fig. 343). When he is in position, I place my left radius across his left carotid and my right ulna across his right carotid and squeeze (fig. 344). This is the ideal position for this hold, but if you happen to be in back of him, it will work just as well with a bit of maneuvering. To make the hold work in this position, you must turn his head to his right. You can do this easily by rolling your forearms across his neck. You can also apply pressure to the back of his head with your own to cause his head to bend forward, thus increasing the pressure (fig. 345).

Figure 341

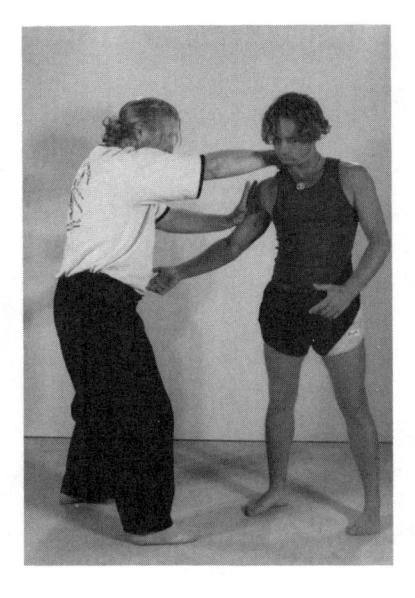

Figure 342

Ultimate Dim-Mak: How to Fight a Grappler and Win

210

Figure 343

Figure 344

The Sleeper Holds

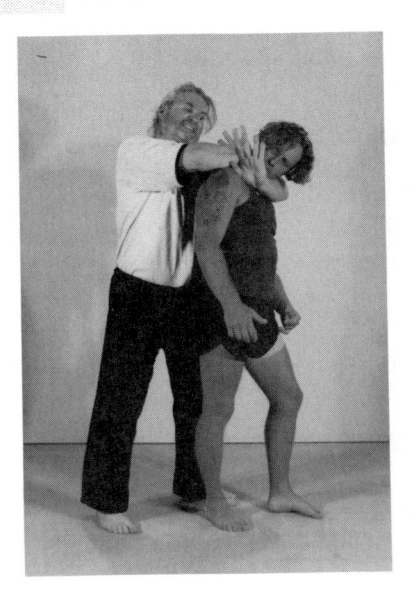

211

Figure 345

TURNING A HEADLOCK INTO A SLEEPER

I have seen too many martial arts magazine covers where some huge bloke with a grim look on his face has someone in an ordinary headlock, as in Figure 346. This type of lock really only wears the captive person down and nothing more, unless it is turned into a sleeper hold.

First, though, we'll talk about the ways to get out of this lock before it is turned into a sleeper. The

Figure 346

main objective here is to turn your head so that your chin is tucked in. You turn your head toward your holder's upper ribs (fig. 347). Now it is relatively easy to grab his left wrist (fig. 348) and violently wrench your head to the rear while jerking his wrist to his rear (fig. 349). Now, a quick step in and you are able to get a reverse figure four or hammer lock and a knee strike to Spleen 19 at his left shoulder, which takes his right leg out (fig. 350). Sp 19 does this by sapping the qi fom the right leg if Sp 19 on his left side is used, and vice versa for the other side.

One of the easiest ways to get out of a headlock is simply to slam your holder in the groin (fig. 351). Or you could try pinching the muscle on the inside of his upper thigh. This never fails to cause him to let go.

In turning a headlock into a sleeper, what the wrists do is important. Rather than just grab him around the neck, you should bend your palm

Figure 347

Figure 348

The Sleeper Holds

213

under his chin (fig. 352). This ensures that he cannot escape. Your right radius is now taking care of his right carotid. The knife edge of your left palm is now placed across his left carotid (fig. 353). Now you squeeze and the blood to the brain is cut off. Again, if he tries to slap you in the groin, you should rip his head off by shaking violently.

Figure 349

Figure 350

Ultimate Dim-Mak: How to Fight a Grappler and Win

214

Figure 351

Figure 352

Figure 353

THE CLASSIC SLEEPER HOLD

This is the hold you see wrestlers using. It is usually applied from the rear and slightly to the side. Your opponent might attack again from the front. You should stun him by slapping him in the neck from the outside, blocking his right arm with your left palm, and moving in on him (fig. 354).

Move quickly around behind him, taking your left forearm around his neck forming a "V" (fig. 355). There are two things you can do with your other palm to increase the pressure on both sides of his neck. One is to take the old "wrestler's grip" with your right palm (fig. 356) and use the power of your right hand to help the left hand squeeze in, thus increasing the "V" on either side of his neck (fig. 357). (Figures 358 and 359 show the wrestler's grip.) The other way is to place your left

Figure 354

Figure 355

palm across your right biceps, taking your right palm over the back of his head (fig. 360). You can use the pressure from your right arm to squeeze tighter, thus pushing your left arm's "V" tighter around both his carotid arteries. You should also use your right palm to turn his head slightly on its side to increase the effect on the arteries (fig. 361).

Figure 356

Figure 357

The Sleeper Holds
217

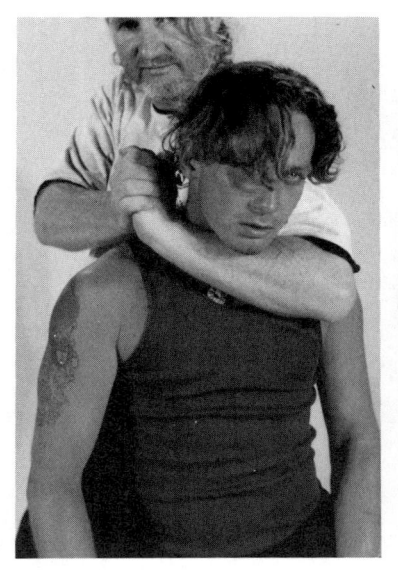

Figure 358

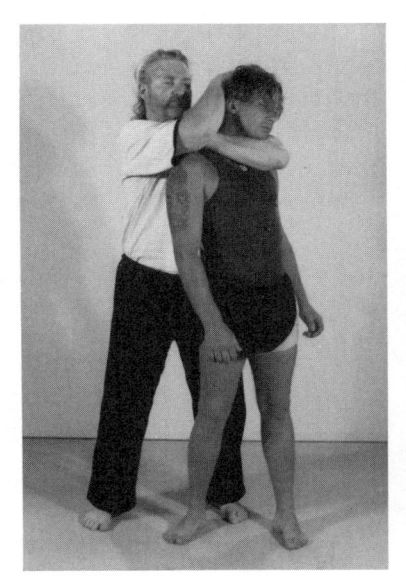

Figure 359

Figure 360

Figure 361

ON THE GROUND OR UP AGAINST A WALL

You might be attacked with a right straight or come straight with both hands. Your right hand slaps your attacker's right forearm toward you as the left palm comes up underneath to take over (fig. 362). Your right palm now slaps him at St 9 point on his right side (fig. 363). He is stunned. Your right foot steps around the back of his right leg, touching it with the back of your right knee. Your right heel is off the ground, while your left palm grabs his right wrist and your right forearm is placed into the inside of his right elbow (fig. 364). Bending his right elbow, you straighten up your right leg, thus kicking his right leg up off the ground. You bend his right elbow and push forward with your right forearm while turning your hips and body to the rear (fig. 365). Throw him to the ground as you follow him down, so that your right knee lands on his right hip (fig. 366). Take

Figure 362

Figure 363

The Sleeper Holds

both fists and place them across his neck, pushing down into the ground to increase the pressure on both of his carotid arteries (fig. 367). This method can also be used against a wall, where he cannot escape. (Perhaps you used the same method of defense when you slapped him at St 9 point, as shown in Figure 368). Now, as he is stunned, push him against a wall, using the crossed-wrist method against his neck (fig. 369).

Of course, it is better not to have to get close enough to need a sleeper hold. Your subconscious attacks should be enough to take him out before he gets close enough to touch you.

Figure 364

Figure 365

Ultimate Dim-Mak: How to Fight a Grappler and Win

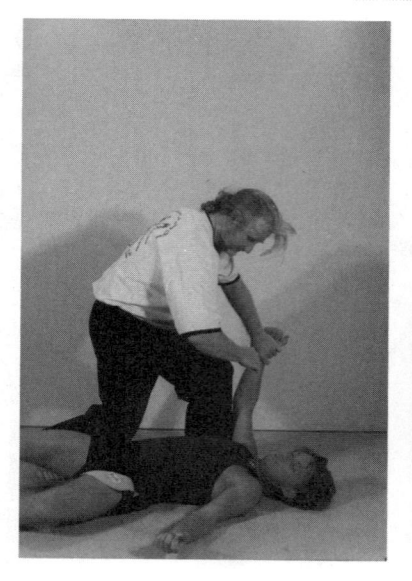

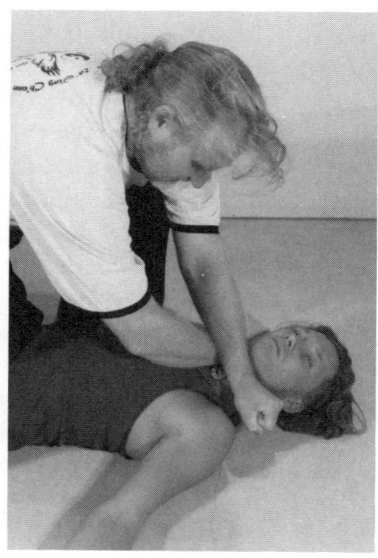

220

Figure 366

Figure 367

Figure 368

Figure 369